Based on a True Story

The American Genocide

Copyright © 2008 E. Slaughter Sr.

ISBN: 978-0-9791461-5-2

All rights reserved. No part of this book may be reproduced or *transmitted* in any form or by any means, electronic or mechanical, including photocopying, recording, or by any information storage and retrieval system, without written permission from the copyright owner.

The American Genocide is an updated and revised version of *Ghosts of Hollandale*- ISBN 978-1419662294 & ISBN 1-59526-519-8.

Library of Congress Control Number: 2008906252

Requests for permission to make copies of any part of this work should be sent to E. Slaughter Sr., PO Box 314, Calumet City, IL 60409

Visit www.slaughter-associates-publishing.com and www.amazon.com to order additional copies.

Printed in the United States of America by Slaughter & Associates

E. Slaughter Sr.

Dedication

This book is dedicated to my mom
and those who treated me like a son—those who have
nurtured and looked over me since childhood:

Willie Mae "Mary" Slaughter (1931-1997)
Willie Mae Barnes (1902-1997)
Mildred Tillis (1916-1998)
and
Nola Bright (1930-2001)

Dedicated, also, to all the tainted blood victims and
a special dedication to Dorothy J. Vanduan

Acknowledgment

I want to thank all of my siblings—especially Sheila, Dorothy, Elaine, Robert, and Jackie—for all they have done for Mom throughout the years, as well as the countless numbers of relatives and friends who gave their support. Special thanks go to Henry and Hubert, who assisted me when this story first came to light in 1998.

Personal Note

I want to express my sincere gratitude to all those who encouraged me to write this story and to those who assisted in typing and pre-editing my manuscript. This book was written not only to bring closure to a dark chapter in my life, but also to illuminate a downplayed issue, hopefully helping one day to completely rid our nation's blood supplies of contaminated blood. To that end, I convey my mother's story. Once you read it, you may understand why it has been reported, "One million Americans are believed to be living with the virus that causes AIDS. Most of them since the 1980s" (AP *Chicago Sun-Times* June 14, 2005).

I believe many were infected after receiving tainted blood transfusions.

Throughout my life, I have felt in tune with the energy of the universe. I have experienced clairvoyance at least five times. In four of these instances, it prevented me from walking into danger. I also believe in the power of words. I believe I was chosen to tell this story long before it occurred. Now I have closure. I kept the story short to bring focus to the importance of the problems of tainted blood and the hope of a possible solution.

To Mother, I love you!

Preface

The *American Genocide* was inspired by the true story of my mother's death. It includes newspaper accounts showing that approximately forty thousand or more people were affected by tainted blood transfusions; many of them are believed to have become sick and died. My mother was among one of those believed to be infected when she was transfused with blood at South Shore and Columbus hospitals in Chicago, Illinois. During the investigation of my mother's death, many questions were asked. How were these people infected and/or killed? Who is at fault? The FDA made a blood recall in December of 1996, although it wasn't publicly announced until December 1998. Why was notification of the recall only brought to the public's eye two years later? Was there a cover-up? Was there a genocide? Were facts regarding my mother's diagnosis and illness suppressed? Did the FDA, New York Blood Center, and Blood Systems Inc. downplay the recall to the media and the American people?

After reviewing the FDA's relevant information concerning the blood companies' involvement, my mother's ordeal, and her medical records, I ask myself—was it a genocide and a cover-up? I am convinced, from the records I have reviewed and my spiritual experiences, that thousands of people died after receiving tainted blood transfusions between 1991 and 1996. I believe the data answered many questions. In this story, I will provide some of those materials.

This story is written in three parts. Part 1 tells of my mother's tragic ordeal, as well as my spiritual encounters—from childhood to adulthood—and information I obtained during the investigation of her death. Part 2, "The Smoking Gun," allows the reader to review the chronology of the account and other relevant facts. Part 3 allows the reader to draw his or her own conclusions to this tragedy. This journal is a testimony of my divine appointment to tell my mom's personal story, which is linked to the worldwide HIV/AIDS epidemic.

Chapter 1

The *American Genocide* is based on a true story. It is the investigational record of my mother's tragic death, which occurred after she was transfused with what was believed to be tainted blood products. The infected blood caused viral infections associated with AIDS, hepatitis, leukemia, sepsis and led, eventually, to death. At one point, I was told that my mother had been diagnosed with, and was being treated for Wegener's granulomatosis. This rare disorder causes inflammation of blood vessels (vasculitis) in the upper respiratory tract (nose, sinuses, and ears), lungs, and kidneys. I later learned that her doctors had prescribed medications that treat not only Wegener's granulomatosis but hepatitis and leukemia as well.

A newspaper article stated that over forty thousand people had been affected in some way by the adulterated blood products, but the victims were never notified; and it wasn't until two years later, in that article, that they discovered the truth.

Many of those infected may have died, and the statute of limitations—a law assigning a certain length of time for prosecution after which rights cannot be enforced by legal action nor offenses punished—had expired by the time the notice appeared in the newspaper. Was it a cover-up, or was it coincidental that a lawsuit claiming a patient had been given tainted blood, contracted AIDS, and eventually died was being heard in the Illinois Supreme Court at the same time?

The following newspaper article and the transcript of a recorded voice mail message from a South Shore Hospital doctor, gives insight into what I believe contributed to my mother's death. It's possible that there are thousands of other victims, which shows the severity of the tainted blood crisis. Evidential documents in part 1 and part 2 of this narrative indicate that the blood supply was tainted before 1994.

Flawed Screening Raises Concerns over Blood Safety

December 2, 1998
(Chicago Tribune)

An estimated thirty-five to forty thousand people may have received tainted blood transfusions or supplies at twenty-eight Chicago-area hospitals between June 1994 and December 1996. The blood may not have been properly tested for HIV or hepatitis viruses.

Four Cities Alerted

The faulty testing was performed by the New York Blood Center, which screens blood for United Blood Services (UBS). While UBS provided blood supplies to hospitals in eighteen states, only blood sent to hospitals in Chicago, Pittsburgh, Memphis, and New York was affected.

What Happened?

1. New York Blood Center technicians exposed blood samples to chemicals that reacted to viral antibodies carried by infected blood.

2. A second test was to be performed using a control sample of chemicals to ensure the testing procedure was accurate.

3. It is believed that the testing lab may not have renewed the control samples frequently enough, putting the accuracy of the entire screening process in doubt.

The flawed procedures were uncovered in late 1996 after an FDA investigation.

Screening Blood

Since 1985, blood is tested for

1. HIV antigen, HIV-1, and HIV-2 (HIV is the virus that causes AIDS);
2. HTLV (a blood-borne virus that can cause leukemia);
3. hepatitis B and hepatitis C (viral infections that cause liver disease).

Samples showing any of these diseases are discarded.

The Illinois Department of Public Health records indicate that over fifteen thousand people were affected with AIDS alone between 1990 and 1999 in the Chicago and Cook County areas. These numbers showed an elevation between 1992 and 1996.

Voice Mail Message:

Mr. Slaughter, this is Dr. — from the laboratory at South Shore Hospital returning your call. I did as much investigating as I could. As I told you before, it doesn't look like we will be able to find out much. LifeSource and the New York Blood Service say there's no way to trace the donor of this particular unit because it happened so long ago and because of the tremendous volume of units affected. It's overwhelming. As I told you before, if you have any questions about the medical situation, you need to talk to your mom's doctor, who I believe you told me was Dr. D— Dr. D—? I can give you his office number: 773-731–. And I did give him your name and number last time we talked. I thought he was going to follow up with a phone call to you. I don't know if he has, or not. But if you have any medical questions, that's who you need to be talking to. Thanks for your callback. See you later.

These incidents are just two of many events. Our family was devastated to learn that Mom had been a possible tainted blood victim. We began to recall incidents at the hospitals that correlated with the tainted blood recall. At that point, I set out to seek the truth and devoted all of the remaining insurance money to that cause.

Could a victim of the tainted blood crisis speak from the grave? I remember my first experience with the supernatural. I believe sharing this episode will allow you to understand how this story unfolded and how my experience with the supernatural granted me an open mind on a subject from which many shy away. It was many years ago, the autumn of 1963, I was about four years old and living in the small southern town of Hollandale, Mississippi. My family toiled as sharecroppers on a plantation. The plantation was adjacent to an old graveyard.

One day, while my family tended the fields, I was walking on a beautiful tree-lined path, picking nuts, when I came upon a godly, soldier-like figure on a horse. Horse and rider were enveloped in a white glow. The rider reached his hand out to me, and I reached out to him. At that moment, I felt a rush of energy go through my body. I was too young to understand what I had encountered, but I never forgot it.

That moment, though brief, was powerful; and the energy of it remained with me throughout my life. The best way to describe it is an adrenaline rush, or what Michael Jordan exhibits when he is in his groove on the basketball court. That same year, my mom decided to leave Hollandale, seeking a better life for us and leaving my father behind. It was a tough decision for her to make. The trip to Chicago was one of the longest car rides of my life, and that holds true to this day. Traveling that dark highway, cramped under my eight siblings, wasn't comfortable. I still recall stopping at restaurants and rest stations and seeing signs that stated Whites Only, Negro Only, and Colored Only. In Chicago, the rugged fields and memories of Hollandale became a piece of history. My mother was delighted. Her desire to protect and provide for us compelled her to become one of the craftiest seamstresses in the city of Chicago, drawing customers to her in droves. She was kindhearted and attractive, and she created many of our dress clothes from scratch. Until her health failed, we met at Mom's home to enjoy great Southern-style, home-cooked meals.

Forty years later, on October 9, 2004, I returned to Hollandale with my eighty-two-year-old uncle so that he might search for his brother whom he hadn't seen in fifty years. It had been a long time since either of us had been home. Several phone calls later, we found my uncle's brother. I returned to that tree-lined path. While the rider did not reappear, I felt that same rush of energy. Often, while investigating my mother's death, this rush of energy led me to facts that would have otherwise escaped me.

In September of 1996, my mother, Mary, was admitted to South Shore Hospital. The doctors said her situation was not serious, but that she did have a heart condition. They indicated that they might have to perform a routine procedure to free one of her heart valves. The cardiologist said my mom would have to undergo a blood transfusion. My sisters and I didn't like the idea, but the cardiologist insisted it was necessary—otherwise, she would continue to weaken.

On October 6 and 7, 1996, Mom was given blood transfusions at South Shore Hospital. On October 8, 1996, she was transferred from South Shore to Columbus Hospital for further testing. Mom almost died that day as bacteria invaded her body and caused an infection. I learned that later, as we, her family, were not given that information at the time. When the doctor told us she needed a transfusion, I felt an energy flood my body, which caused me to resist his suggestion. But the doctor insisted and ultimately prevailed, and the procedure was done. In retrospect, I wish I had continued to resist. When the infection set in, Mom's cardiologist, Dr. Tyson, and her attending physician, Dr. Dayon, appeared as shocked and surprised as we were that she had taken a turn for the worse. One of my sisters stayed with her at the hospital, but those of us with less-accommodating employers had to be satisfied with visiting Mom daily until she was discharged. We were told that Mom had a disease called Wegener's granulomatosis. This was hard to believe as it is rare in African-Americans; but her symptoms, including kidney failure, fit the disease.

On January 18, 1997, Mom was admitted to St. Margaret's Hospital in Hammond, Indiana, and referred to a clinic for dialysis. She underwent many tests while there. The test results revealed she had a *Staphylococcus aureus* bacterial infection, a dangerous condition because it is resistant to antibiotics. Although Mom continued to receive dialysis and treatment for Wegener's granulomatosis, her condition worsened. It seemed odd that the other infections identified earlier weren't detected at St. Margaret's Hospital, but perhaps they were suppressed by the medications she was taking. A short time later, she was admitted to South Suburban Hospital in Hazelcrest, Illinois. At South Suburban, the doctors were puzzled by her condition. The attending physicians were from Columbus Hospital, where she had received some of her blood transfusions. I became suspicious when a doctor told me, after I asked about her extended stay, that some of her medical expenses were being paid for by another source. Believing the charges were being paid by one of her previous doctors, I attempted to locate the source, but was unsuccessful.

On March 24, 1997, while on my way to work, a notion came over me to check in on Mom. I detoured from my route and went to South Suburban. The staff was very courteous and allowed me immediate access. When I got off the elevator, a strange feeling came over me, and I hurried to her room, expecting the worst. She was sitting up in bed, smiling, and seasoning her lunch. I hadn't seen her that energetic in months! "Mom, how are you?" I asked.

"I'm great. The doctor said if I eat well, I can go home tomorrow."

"Oh, really?" I said.

I was stunned to see how happy she looked. She was glowing in her neat two-piece pajama set. I was amazed, but it felt so good to see her looking well that I believed she was going to be all right. I had to get to work, so I gave Mom a hug and a kiss on the cheek, and I told her I loved her. I went to work feeling great.

Early the next day, before sunrise, on March 25, 1997, the telephone rang. It was my sister. She said, "The hospital called and said Mom isn't doing so well. We need to get there right away." I sensed what was about to happen, but I wanted to think positively. I was hoping for the best. When I arrived at the hospital thirty minutes later, I went numb at the sound of people crying in my mother's room.

Mom was gone. As we all wept around her lifeless body, I felt her spirit near me. We all knew the pain she had endured since being hospitalized at South Shore. While we were relieved that her suffering was over, the question lingered in our minds, why did our mother die?

Who, or what, alerted me to visit Mother the day before she died? Did she know she was going to die? She had said, "I am going home tomorrow." What did she mean by "going home"?

A few days after my mother's funeral, I received a letter saying I had been accepted into Cooley Law School. I was very happy but felt sad because although my mother had attended my high school and college graduations, she would never see me graduate from law school—a goal I had been working toward for several years. Two months later, I received a promotion at my job. However, my mother's death left me unable to take much pleasure in that either. Then, oddly enough, I found myself attending more than twenty additional funerals, and my daughter had to have back surgery that summer.

While she was learning to walk again, I decided to prioritize my life. At that moment, my family was more important than school. I put off studying law for the time being. Instead, I used money that would have been spent for law school to finance my children's educations. I was so happy when 1997 ended; I had never had a year like it before. Some good things had happened; but losing my mother, having my daughter undergo back surgery, and dealing with so much death caused me to hope things would get better.

Chapter 2

Early in the morning of December 2, 1998, I awoke from a dream and saw a beautiful full moon shining through the window. A familiar rush of energy surged through me, and gazing at the moon, I remembered my dream. I knew something important would be in the newspaper that morning, but I didn't really understand what was going on and fell back to sleep. I woke again around seven thirty. I got my two daughters up for school and then went outside to retrieve the newspaper. I took it with me to the kitchen where my coffee was waiting. The headline stunned me: "Years Later, 40,000 Warned of Possible Transfusion Risk."

As I read the story, the mystery of my mother's death became clear. The article listed the years when people were infected and the hospitals where the individuals involved had been treated. Sure enough, South Shore and Columbus, where my mother had received her transfusions, were among those included. I immediately went to South Shore Hospital and demanded my mother's medical records. I then ordered the records from Columbus Hospital. After receiving and reviewing them, it seemed clear that Mom had become sick after her blood transfusions. According to her records, she had suffered more severely at Columbus than at South Shore.

Mom had received blood transfusions on November 6, 9, 10, 13, and 15, 1996, at Columbus Hospital. It was possible that she had received contaminated blood during those transfusions that would explain her relapses. Were the doctors unaware that the blood was polluted, or did they know and performed the multiple blood transfusions to try to cleanse her body of tainted blood? The newspaper stated the blood products concerned were administered between 1994 and 1996. However, the severity of the problem went back to New York and the consent decree as it is quoted. An FDA report —dated February 10, 1997—called *A Consent Decree Correspondence* stated, "Because of the serious nature of improper testing, the FDA has no assurance that blood samples from September 1, 1991, through November 20, 1996, were properly tested." If the newspaper's account was off by three years, all the calculations were off. Over one hundred thousand people may have been involved.

Another letter—dated January 14, 1997—stated, "Appropriate follow-up, i.e. recall, should be conducted on blood products from donors for which samples cannot be obtained for retesting." An FDA article dated December 29, 1993, stated, "Greater New York Blood Program Recalls Blood Products." The FDA had received inquiries concerning a recall of blood products by the Greater New York Blood Program in New York City. The blood products— which initially tested reactive for the HIV antibody, the virus that causes AIDS —were not tested in duplicate as required by the manufacturer's testing instructions and FDA regulations. "The recalled blood products were collected on March 15, 1987, and included red blood cells, platelets (cryoprecipitate blood component used to aid clotting), and recovered plasma. The donor responded that he had tested HIV-1 positive in April 1992."

It appears that the tainted blood problems began well before 1994. It was understandable that they did not want to alarm the public, but it was their duty to inform those who received dirty transfused blood. While the FDA and NYBC communicated their concerns to one another, the blood supplier and owner of the blood products sent to the hospitals did not alert the individuals or the public in a timely manner. One assumes that there were many reasons, but none would be a viable excuse. The *Advincula* case, which was being appealed in the Illinois Supreme Court, makes one think it was all about money. That case concerned an individual infected with tainted blood and was being heard when the consent decree was filed, announcing a recall of the tainted blood products. The *Chicago Tribune* ran the article almost two years later, stating that approximately forty thousand people may also have been infected by tainted blood before the recall. If the recall had been made public in a timely manner—right after November 20, 1996—it would have given that pending case a boost. Other lawsuits might have followed, but because of the late recall, the statute of limitations was running out for many potential victims. It would have been a shattering blow to the blood banks, the hospitals, doctors, nurses, and blood donors. The clock was ticking for me.

I began contacting lawyers about my suspicions and was told that the statute of limitations would soon run out. If I wanted to take legal action against the hospitals, I would have to file a complaint by March 25, 1999.

As I prepared my case, I encountered many inexplicable events. I uncovered an interesting fact from the Illinois Department of Public Health: In 1981, only four cases of AIDS were reported. According to their documents, an additional twenty-six thousand AIDS cases had been reported between the years 1982 and 2001. Some were related to tainted blood transfusions, and the majority came from the Chicago area. From 1990 to 1999, 15,643 cases of AIDS had been reported in Cook County and Chicago.

During the tainted blood crisis between 1990 and 1996, there had been an escalation of AIDS cases. In 1990, 942 cases were reported, rising in 1994 to 2,462 and dropping to 962 in 1998. The Illinois Department of Public Health printed statistics on *Reportable Communicable Disease Cases, 1990-1999*, which lists hepatitis A in 1990 at 1,726 cases and in 1999 at 849 cases. It also states that hepatitis B was at 591 cases in 1990 and at a low of 213 cases in 1999. There was an increase in diseases associated with hepatitis and AIDS/HIV in Cook County during the consent decree era. The hepatitis numbers also decreased dramatically after the 1996 blood recall. I wrote a letter to the Illinois Department of Public Health requesting an investigation of my mother's death and the blood contamination. In a letter dated April 20, 2001, they responded.

Dear Mr. Slaughter:

Director John R. Lumpkin, M.D. has asked me to respond to your letter of March 14, 2001 regarding complaint number 00-2448. A review of your complaint has determined that it should be investigated under the Illinois Hospital Licensing Act [210 ILCS 85].

As of July 15, 2007, I have not received a resolution of my complaints and inquiries. I have made several attempts to learn the status of my request, but to no avail. The statistics should have encouraged the Illinois Department of Public Health to investigate my complaint.

As I continued to investigate the cause of Mom's death, I became more and more convinced that it was related to the blood transfusions and not a heart condition. Her medical records, blood tests, and the kidney biopsy, along with advice from a medical professional, supported my belief.

I became more determined to take legal action against the hospitals and those responsible. I met with many attorneys between December 1998 and March 1999, attempting to find someone who would take the case. All of the firms I contacted declined. They said it was because of the complexity of the case and the lack of time in which to prepare before the statute of limitations ran out. I spent hundreds of hours researching legal opinions and documents related to my case. As March approached, my energy levels elevated. Often, while researching, I would feel a rush of energy; and then out of the blue, I'd locate an item that proved very important in supporting my theory. I logged hundreds of hours at public and law libraries, seeking answers and guidance on how to prepare the case myself if I were unable to retain a lawyer in time. I believed that many of the attorneys I approached feared taking on the blood bank's attorneys.

Chapter 3

On March 23, 1999, two days before the expiration of the statute of limitations, I filed a complaint in the United States District Court, Northern District of Illinois Eastern Division. It was assigned case number 99 C 1888; I felt like a new attorney filing his first case.

While putting the case together, it felt like unknown forces were guiding me. However, as the first court date approached, I was still looking for an attorney to represent me. A small number of attorneys considered taking on the case, but I could not wait for them. I had to make sure all of the defendants in my case were properly served with summons. After I had the defendants served, I contacted an attorney who had been handling a real estate matter for me, and I told him about the case I had filed.

A few days later, he told me he was interested in handling the case. He assured me that he had handled these types of cases before, and he appeared excited about it. He filed his appearance with the federal court so he would appear as the attorney of record. I didn't think anything was out of the ordinary until one night, a few days before our court appearance in May of 1999, a message was sent to me in a dream, telling me that this lawyer had dismissed the real estate case he was handling for me without my knowledge. This message, I believe, was warning me that my current case was in jeopardy as well. It appeared transcendental, and when I later doubted this dream, a physical object actually moved by itself. A calendar fell off the wall for no discernable reason. I was baffled and somewhat fearful of what I'd seen. After checking with the courts, I learned that the lawyer had dismissed the real estate case in 1998. I was even more baffled and became very angry. My attorney, Mr. Jordan, had called me in February of 1999, indicating on a voice mail message that the real estate case was to go on trial soon.

At that point, I knew there was something to my dreams. I decided not to tell Mr. Jordan that I knew about the case dismissal until I met him in court the following day. I did not want any more surprises.

I arrived early at the federal court building to ensure that everything was on track. I wore a blue suit and carried a black briefcase. I looked more like an attorney than my lawyer. At nine thirty in the morning, we were in court. A few minutes later, the clerk called my case, *Slaughter v. New York Blood Center et al.* There were about twenty-two people sitting in the courtroom, and except for four people, they all stood and approached the bench. I was amazed that all the defendants' lawyers had appeared. Some defendants had two lawyers representing their doctors and hospitals. I knew I was in for a legal battle. I had a choice to make—to quit or to keep fighting. I had spent almost all of the remaining insurance money on this case, and I had a lawyer I didn't trust. My mind wandered as the judge spoke and the attorneys answered. They spelled their names for the court reporter. One defense lawyer, wearing a very expensive suit, looked toward me and attempted to intimidate me by saying aloud, "I am going to blow this case away." He stared directly at me for about ten seconds. I was on the verge of quitting, feeling powerless fighting all of these defendants alone; but instead I said, "Oh, God, please help me." I began to feel strong again; his attempts to intimidate me only encouraged me to keep fighting. From then on, I never feared the defendants or felt intimidated again.

When the attorneys finished speaking, the judge said, "I know the motions to dismiss will be many, so please don't wait until the last minute." He set the next status hearing for June 16, 1999. I sat down to gather my thoughts and asked myself, "Why didn't I fire this attorney while at the bench?"

As I left the courtroom, I saw my attorney down the hall, in a quiet corner, talking with a few of the defendants' lawyers. I was too upset to approach him, but it appeared from their facial expressions that they didn't want me to know what they were discussing. I then believed my dream entirely. My attorney had told me I didn't have to appear and that he would handle everything. Had "handling everything" included selling out? My attorney's actions were now obvious.

A few days later, my attorney told me he needed some money for working on this case. I told him we needed to meet and change our agreement. While at his office, I presented him with an agreement that said, "Our agreement was on a contingency basis when you took over this case." Why was he suddenly asking for money? It was a surprise to me, especially when he knew I was aware of the contingency agreement. Attorney Jordan quickly signed the agreement and asked, "Do you have a check for me?" I told him I would call him later and quickly left his office.

On June 15, 1999, I received a call from the federal court stating there would be no court on June 16, 1999. The judge dismissed the case for lack of jurisdiction in federal court, which extended my statute of limitation by one year. I began to feel more powerful. My prayer, spoken in the courtroom, had been answered. I now had one year to refile the case in the Illinois circuit court in Cook County. Attorney Jordan, realizing I was onto his game, filed a motion to remove himself from the case; but the judge stated that in his opinion, it was a moot issue because the case had been dismissed. I began to feel strong again. I met with several lawyers and eventually signed a new deal with one of them.

This lawyer was crafty. He was so impressed by my investigation into the tainted blood supplies and my court filings that he attempted to put me on his payroll. He had me investigate an asbestos case. I would receive a percentage if the case was settled or won in court.

I later decided to have my first attorney, Mr. Jordan, investigated by the Illinois Attorney Registration and Disciplinary Commission (ARDC) for dismissing my real estate case without permission. However, he convinced the ARDC that he had done it with my full knowledge. I was bitter that he had gotten away with it, but I learned a great deal about him. I also had the doctor and cardiologist investigated. I knew that unless I could conclusively establish that the blood was tainted, it would be very difficult to prove any wrongdoing by the doctors and the hospitals. I continued to research medical records, court documents, and FDA documents, hoping that the Illinois Department of Public Health would initiate their own investigation and provide a finding that would be useful to me. I continued to write to the Illinois Department of Public Health, and they repeated that it was under investigation. It became obvious, after a while, that they were not looking into it seriously. They said they would, but did they? I knew I would have to refile my complaint within a few months; the filing deadline was quickly approaching.

My new attorney told me he would handle it. Looking back at his actions, I believe he had planned to watch me work; he never intended to file. As the date neared, I reminded my attorney about the statute of limitations. We met at his office more often. Still he did nothing, and I eventually terminated his services.

A month before I had to refile, in a low mood, I contacted the blood supplier and asked if they wanted to settle the case. I informed the company's lawyer, who was also their vice president, that I had fired my attorney and was representing myself. A few days later, I received a written offer of $10,000 to settle the case. I knew that if I took the money, no further legal action against any of the defendants would be possible. I almost took it; I could have recovered some of the money I had spent preparing the case.

After sleeping on it, I decided not to accept. This story had to be told one day, and I would have been letting my mom and the other victims down. I told the blood supplier's attorney that I was not taking his offer. I filed the case pro se in the circuit court and began to search for another attorney. Like the rest I had contacted, they thought the case was too much work, with no guarantees. I wasn't about to do what I had done in the federal court, which was serve all the defendants and be in the same position all over again. I continued to pressure the Illinois Department of Public Health and search court records.

I was surfing the Internet when I found a very interesting case. A wrongful death case involving a blood transfusion had been appealed to the Illinois Supreme Court. There was a lot of bad press about Justice Freeman, who wrote the opinion—something to do with donations and appointments to the bench. It appeared the medical and justice systems were flawed.

Former governor, George Ryan, of Illinois was indicted in December 2003 on unrelated charges, which made me more skeptical. Was the state going to investigate my complaint about the tainted blood and the recall? It was also imperative to note that former vice chairman of the Health Facilities Planning Board, Stewart Levine, who had been appointed by Governor Ryan, was indicted in May 2005, accused of leveraging his post on the board of health so two of his associates could get lucrative hospital construction and financing contracts. He was also a key fund-raiser for the attorney general, who lost his bid to replace the indicted governor. I called the lawyer who handled the case in the Illinois Supreme Court and asked if she was familiar with the tainted blood scare in New York that had affected the Chicagoland area or United Blood Services and the consent decree that had been signed around the time the Illinois Supreme Court heard her case. She said no. Maybe the recall announcement had been delayed to allow that case to proceed, not letting the plaintiff learn of the tainted blood or decree. If the blood recall had appeared in the newspapers in 1996, the justice's opinion might have been different and opened up a floodgate of lawsuits. By waiting two years, the statute of limitations was over for many, and most of the victims would have died.

It appeared "something" or "someone" was leading me to more and more information. If I hadn't believed in the supernatural and hadn't had that earlier experience with the spirit in Hollandale, maybe my mind would have been closed. I would not have followed up on, or trusted in, any of the dreams or hunches that led me to facts and documents that helped me to investigate this case—such as the property case dismissal. Were the hospitals and blood bank responsible for a massacre? If so, then it was a devastating event. Was there a cover-up? I don't know. Review the FDA Consent Decree, the FDA summary of findings, and other related material, and decide for yourself. The answers to some questions may be found within these documents. I am convinced, from what I have read and reviewed, that there was a massacre, a cover-up, and that similar problems occurred elsewhere in this country without the public's knowledge.

Next, I provide a recap and the chronological order of facts and events, detailing relevant information. This data convinced me that something terrible happened to my mom and to thousands of other people because of receiving tainted blood transfusions.

Chapter 4

The Smoking Gun

The Smoking Gun is the chronological order of events that will further explain what caused Mom's death. I refer to her at times as Mary. A terrible tragedy occurred when hospitals around the country administered tainted blood. It led to indictments and the firing of high-ranking employees at the New York Blood Center. The news appeared in the papers roughly two years after the fact, in the form of a blood recall in the Chicagoland area, where approximately forty thousand people may have been contaminated. I believe there were motives for a cover-up, and I have documented some of the events that took place. I recount public information, documents from the courts, FDA statistics, as well as my mother's medical records. This section contains what might be referred to as the "smoking gun."

Documentation and Chronological Order of Events

As I enter into this phase of the story, my intentions are not only to tell my personal story but also to shed light on events that helped create *The American Genocide*.

I have received and reviewed much data and will now present the materials that directly and indirectly affected my mother. I believe all the information is important, and that these facts expose items that are of significance to my mother and thousands of others. I present it in its entirety, so nothing is discounted or misquoted. This section will also present facts that will give you a clear view of the problems associated with the blood supply in this country, specifically in the Memphis, Pittsburgh, New York, and the Chicagoland areas. I will detail how many people may have been affected, my attempt to file a class action lawsuit, and situations that may indicate that there was a cover-up. I will also cover coincidental and/or suspicious activities during the recall of 1996.

***

This is a chronological order of events. It provides details of the companies and people involved, including documents that support various assertions. Many of the documents presented are summarized with names, dates, and titles; a short explanation may follow some of the documents.

Note: This section reads like a police report. My intention is to present the papers so that you may envision events as they are.

A few points in this section are a recapitulation of facts. This section will also help explain why I believe my mom was an ultimate sacrifice to expose a genocide and cover-up that is linked to the worldwide HIV/AIDS epidemic.

December 29, 1993

T 93-51

Document titled **"Greater New York Blood Program Recalls Blood Products"**

The FDA has been receiving inquiries concerning a recall of blood products by the Greater New York Blood Program in New York City. The recall was undertaken because the blood products, which initially tested reactive for antibodies to HIV, the virus that causes AIDS, were not retested in duplicate as required by the manufacturer's testing instructions and FDA regulations.

Author's aside: *The blood in question was collected on March 15, 1987, and later transfused into a patient. The donor stated he had tested positive for anti-HIV-1 in 1992. The recipient later tested positive for anti-HIV-1. As part of this recall, doctors were able to locate both the donor and recipient of this blood. It was obvious then that the blood supply was tainted; it is important to note that both the donor and recipient were notified during the recall. Why was my mother and many others not notified during the 1996 recall?*

April 22, 1994

Document from the FDA to United Blood Services of Chicago and Blood Systems, Inc.:

The Food and Drug Administration (FDA or the agency) conducted an inspection of United Blood Services Systems Inc. (1221 North LaSalle, Chicago, Illinois) between September 20, 1993, and February 2, 1994. During this inspection, an FDA investigator documented numerous significant deviations from the applicable standards and requirements of subchapter F, parts 600–680, title 21, Code of Federal Regulations and the applicable standards in your license (first paragraph of page 1). If you choose not to bring your establishment into compliance and wish to waive the opportunity of a hearing, then you must contact the acting director, Office of Compliance, within ten (10) days of receipt of this letter. The waiver must be confirmed in writing and may be accomplished by your voluntary request that U.S. license 0183-023 be revoked" (last paragraph of page 6).

DEPARTMENT OF HEALTH & HUMAN SERVICES　　　　Public Health Service

April 22, 1994

Food and Drug Administration
Center for Biologics Evaluation and Research
1401 Rockville Pike
Rockville MD 20852-1448

CERTIFIED - RETURN RECEIPT REQUESTED

Ernest R. Simon, M.D.
Responsible Head
United Blood Services
 Blood Systems, Inc.
6210 East Oak Street
P.O. Box 1867
Scottsdale, AZ 85252

Dear Dr. Simon:

The Food and Drug Administration (FDA or the agency) conducted an inspection of United Blood Services Blood Systems, Inc., 1221 North LaSalle, Chicago, Illinois, between September 20, 1993, and February 2, 1994. During the inspection, an FDA investigator documented numerous significant deviations from the applicable standards and requirements of Subchapter F, Parts 600-680, Title 21, Code of Federal Regulations and the applicable standards in your license. The deviations noted on the Form FDA-483, Inspectional Observations, issued at the conclusion of the inspection, include, but are not limited to, the following:

1. Failure to adequately determine donor suitability, [21 CFR 640.32(b) and 640.65(b)(1)(i)], in that total protein and protein electrophoresis determinations were not performed on at least three donors of Fresh Frozen Plasma by apheresis.

2. Failure to establish scientifically sound and appropriate specifications, standards, and test procedures to assure that blood and blood components are safe, pure, potent, and effective. For example, the inspection revealed that at least four donors who had previously tested repeatedly reactive for the antibody to the human immunodeficiency virus type 1 (anti-HIV-1) were not appropriately reentered. [21 CFR 606.140(a) and 610.45(c)]

3. Failure to use supplies and reagents in a manner consistent with the manufacturer's instructions, [21 CFR 606.65(e)], in that the investigator observed incorrect volumes of conjugate reagent were added while performing antibody to hepatitis B core antigen (anti-HBc) and antibody to hepatitis C virus encoded antigen (anti-HCV) testing. The investigator observed a technician dispense conjugate from a multi-channel pipette into microwells with varying and inconsistent volumes. Even though the volume of conjugate required by the manufacturer's instructions is 200ul, a

Author's aside: *It is obvious that there were problems with certain blood suppliers in the Chicago area as well as New York. The problems were so bad in Chicago that the FDA threatened to revoke the supplier's licenses.*

May 6, 1994

Document from Blood Systems, Inc. to FDA:

We are extremely concerned about the compliance issues in FDA 483 and the letter from Dr. Zoon, and we are taking aggressive steps to correct and monitor deficiencies to achieve long-term compliance in Chicago. We are available to meet CBER and/or the Chicago District Office, if such a meeting would be beneficial (two-page document, last paragraph of page 1).

THE AMERICAN GENOCIDE

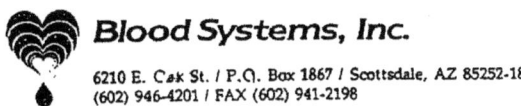

Blood Systems, Inc.

6210 E. Oak St. / P.O. Box 1867 / Scottsdale, AZ 85252-1867
(602) 946-4201 / FAX (602) 941-2198

May 6, 1994

James Simmons
Acting Director
Office of Compliance, HFM-600
CBER
Suite 300N
1401 Rockville Pike
Rockville, MD 20852-1448

Dear Mr. Simmons:

We received Dr. Kathryn Zoon's letter of intent to revoke the license at Blood Systems, Inc. dba United Blood Services, 1221 La Salle, Chicago, IL on April 28, 1994. We have taken several steps to correct the deficiencies noted by the Food and Drug Administration (FDA) including, retraining by both Abbott and Ortho representatives in the viral marker area and the corrective actions addressed in our response to the FDA483 (**Attachment A**). In addition the following actions will be or have been taken by BSI:

- Operations Plan of Action - This plan addresses short and long term actions to be taken to bring the Chicago facility into and maintain compliance. (**Attachment B**)

- Short and Long Term Plan of Action-Technical Compliance - A 3-day shut down of the Chicago facility and its satellite centers will occur May 20-22, 1994 to conduct internal retraining. The plan also includes long term support for this center over the next 6 months to monitor compliance and take additional action as required. It will be used during the retraining on May 20-22, 1994. (**Attachment C**)

- Irradiation Memo - This is the most recent revision of the SOP on Irradiation. The FDA 483 issues are addressed. (**Attachment D**)

- The Quality/Compliance Relationship 4/94 - A video was prepared for all BSI staff. The video will be shown during the 3 day retraining. (**Attachment E**)

- Consultants Initial Report on BSI Ethics/Compliance - BSI is currently working with the consulting firm, Strategic Management Systems, Inc., to assist with BSI's ethics/compliance needs. (**Attachment F**)

July 17–September 25, 1995

Title: **EI JMM**

United Blood Service
Chicago, IL
CFN 1471471

Summary of findings: forty pages and five inspectional observation pages, FDA findings

I conducted a directed inspection of this licensed blood bank as defined in the May 18, 1995, assignment (attached no. 1), which provides for a coordinated approach to reinspection of United Blood Services (UBS) facilities, following the notice of intent to revoke license letter. Inspection was conducted in accordance with CP 7342.001A.

Inspection of Licensed Blood Banks and AIDS Pac 42R825

(paragraph 1, page 1)

The previous inspection of this facility was conducted September 20, 1993–February 2, 1994. At the conclusion of the inspection, a seventy-point FDA-483 was issued to the firm's management, citing deviations to include collection of blood from unsuitable individuals and reinstatement of ineligible HIV-reactive donors (page 1, last paragraph).

The laboratory department at this facility has significantly reduced its activity since the previous inspection. Donor testing (HIV, HTLV-I, hepatitis, syphilis, and ABO/Rh/Ab screen) was discontinued on UBS products in June

1994 and transferred to New York Blood Center (NYBC). Ms. Suwe reports the Chicago test results are transferred from NYBC to UBS-Scottsdale upon completion. Upon receipt in Scottsdale, test results are downloaded to Chicago, via BBOSS, to allow product labeling (page 8, last paragraph).

```
EI JMM                          1             UNITED BLOOD SERVICES
7/17 - 9/25/95                                CHICAGO, IL
                                              CFN 1471471
SUMMARY OF FINDINGS:
```

I conducted a directed inspection of this licensed blood bank as defined in the 5/18/95 assignment (Attachment No. 1), which provides for a coordinated approach to reinspection of United Blood Services (UBS) facilities, following the **Notice of Intent to Revoke License Letter**. Inspection was conducted in accordance with C.P. 7342.001A, "Inspection of Licensed Blood Banks" and AIDS Pac 42R825.

United Blood Services-Chicago (UBS Chicago) collects approximately [ ] units, of blood annually and supplies products, under contract to [ ] Chicagoland hospitals. UBS Chicago includes the LaSalle Street .location and nine satellite donor centers. The LaSalle Street location (subject of the current inspection), maintains a whole blood/hemapheresis donor room, component preparation area, a limited laboratory operation, and a distribution department.

Since the previous inspection several significant operational changes have occurred at this facility:

* In June, 1994, testing on UBS units (disease markers, ABO/Rh, Ab screen) was discontinued and transferred to the New York Blood Center. UBS/Chicago continued to test donor blood under contract for local unlicensed blood banks until August 6, 1995.

* UBS discontinued reinstatement of donors who previously tested positive for HIV or Hepatitis. Reportedly, this policy has been discontinued at UBS centers nationwide.

* "Lookback" and STTD (suspect transfusion transmitted disease) investigations are no longer conducted in Chicago. Information is reportedly transferred to the firm's corporate office, Scottsdale AZ, for review and corrective action.

* Management at the firm has changed since the previous inspection. As of the conclusion of the inspection Mr. Charles Grossenbacher had replaced Toby Simon, M.D. as Responsible Head of UBS. Locally, W. Howie Walz had been replaced as the Executive Director of UBS Chicago by Acting Executive Director, Michael Anania.

The previous inspection of this facility was conducted 9/20/93-2/2/94. At the conclusion of the inspection a 70-point FDA-483 was issued to firm's management citing deviations to include:

E. SLAUGHTER SR.

Author's aside: *This report also states that unlicensed local blood banks continued to collect blood for United Blood Services, also known as UBS. Duplicate donor problems existed in their Scottsdale, Arizona, office computer files. In addition, there were over forty pages of violations found in the United Blood Services laboratory located in Chicago.*

Chapter 5

September 26, 1996

While at work, I received a call from my sister, who lived in the same condominium complex as my mother. She said, "The ambulance is here to get Mom. She was having problems breathing. I think they are taking her to South Shore Hospital."

I left work and headed for South Shore. As I passed Mom's building, I spotted ambulance number 50 outside. I approached the ambulance and observed her inside, receiving oxygen. She moved her head in acknowledgment of the EMT's commands. I knocked on the window of the ambulance and said, "Why are you all still here? Take my mom to the hospital now." They sped off, and I followed them to the hospital where she was moved to the emergency room. She was later admitted.

Discharge Summary

Patient: Mary

Admitted to South Shore Hospital, September 26, 1996. Disposition: On October 8, 1996, at 7:45 p.m., patient was transferred to Columbus Hospital via ambulance. Copy of chart was sent. The patient was not in acute distress. The patient left the hospital going to Columbus in fair condition.

Principal Diagnosis: Congestive heart failure

Secondary Diagnosis: none

Principal Procedures: Packed cell transfusion on October 6 by Dr. Cullins.

Cardiologist: Dr. Tyson's recommendations

Consultation with Dr. Cullins

Impression: Cardiomyopathy

Author's aside: Mom was transfused with blood products on October 6 and October 7, 1996, while at South Shore Hospital. Our family was against the blood transfusion, but Dr. Tyson insisted it was necessary.

October 8, 1996

Mom was admitted to Columbus Hospital. On this day, her health declined rapidly. Infections, hematuria, uremia, and bacteria were detected in her body by medical staff.

November 1, 1996

A kidney biopsy revealed an infection diagnosed as glomerulonephritis, a condition that causes renal failure and which is brought on by an acute nephritic syndrome from viruses and infections.

November 6, 9, 10, 11, 13, and 15, 1996

Mom received blood transfusions of one unit of blood on each of these days at Columbus. She then suffered additional severe infections and was placed on antibiotics and dialysis. (I believe the blood transfusions and dialysis may have been performed to attempt to eradicate the infections found in the biopsy and other tests.)

November 19, 1996

Adulterated blood was reported to have stopped flowing into the hospitals.

November 20, 1996

Mom was discharged with a diagnosis of Wegener's granulomatosis.

December 17, 1996

Title: Consent Decree U.S. District Court SD of NY (41 pages total)

United States of America,
Plaintiff

v.

New York Blood Center Inc. et al.,
Defendants

The defendants must do the following: prompt, thorough, and documented investigation of all adverse reactions, suspected transfusion-associated infection, and HIV lookback. Prompt quarantine of potentially unsuitable blood products, documentation of disposition of unsuitable blood products, and prompt notification of consignees; prompt recall of unsuitable blood products and prompt notification to consignees including, but not limited to, hospitals, customers, subconsignees, distributors, brokers, and fractionators; review of manufacturing records as part of investigations of HIV lookback and suspected transfusion-associated infection cases, including records identified as containing alleged errors (pages 18 and 19).

If defendants violate this consent decree and are found in civil or criminal contempt thereof, NYBC shall, in addition to other remedies, reimburse the United States for its attorney's fees, investigational expenses, and court costs relating to such contempt proceedings (page 37, XIII).

This consent decree shall be binding upon NYBC's successors, assignees, and affiliates, excluding VI Technologies (page 38, XV).

MARY JO WHITE
United States Attorney for the
Southern District of New York
By: DEBORAH Y. YEOH (DY-5165)
Assistant United States Attorney
100 Church Street, 19th Floor
New York, New York 10007
Tel. No.: (212) 385-6365

UNITED STATES DISTRICT COURT
SOUTHERN DISTRICT OF NEW YORK
- - - - - - - - - - - - - - - - -x

UNITED STATES OF AMERICA,   :

        Plaintiff,   :

  against   :   CONSENT DECREE

NEW YORK BLOOD CENTER, INC.,   :   96 Civ. 9464 (RH)
JOHN ADAMSON, M.D.,
CELSO BIANCO, M.D., and   :
JENNI LEE ROBINS,
                                   :
        Defendants.
                                   :
- - - - - - - - - - - - - - - - -x

PATTERSON, J.

ORIGINAL

U.S. DISTRICT COURT
FILED
DEC 17 1996
S.D. OF N.Y.

WHEREAS, plaintiff United States of America, on behalf of the United States Food and Drug Administration (the "FDA"), has filed a Complaint against New York Blood Center, Inc. ("NYBC"), a not-for-profit corporation incorporated in and doing business in the State of New York, and against individual defendants John Adamson, M.D., President and Chief Executive Officer; Celso Bianco, M.D., Vice President of Medical Affairs; and Jenni Lee Robins, Vice President of Blood Operations and Responsible Head (collectively, "Defendants"), seeking permanent injunctive relief pursuant to the Federal Food, Drug, and

December 19, 1996

Justice Charles E. Freeman, of the Illinois Supreme Court, delivered an opinion in the case of *Advincula v. United Blood Services*. In summary, the plaintiff brought suit after her husband died of AIDS, contracted in 1984 through blood supplied by United Blood Services. It is an undisputed fact that the donor of the blood that Advincula received had tested positive for HIV in 1986 and that this blood was the source of the infection. After a lengthy trial, the plaintiff won 2.14 million dollars in damages. The defendant, United Blood Services (UBS), appealed the decision. The defendant won the appeal before the Illinois Appellate Court. The plaintiff appealed the consequent ruling with the Illinois Supreme Court, which then remanded the case for a retrial under the two-step standard:

1. An examination of the professional standards of the blood banking industry.

2. Analysis under general "due care," which can only be breached if industry standards were found deficient.

The American Genocide

NOTICE: Under Supreme Court Rule 367 a party has 21 days after the filing of the opinion to request a rehearing. Also, opinions are subject to modification, correction or withdrawal at anytime prior to issuance of the mandate by the Clerk of the Court. Therefore, because the following slip opinion is being made available prior to the Court's final action in this matter, it cannot be considered the final decision of the Court. The official copy of the following opinion will be published by the Supreme Court's Reporter of Decisions in the Official Reports advance sheets following final action by the Court.

Docket No. 79653--Agenda 12--January 1996.
MARIETTA ADVINCULA, Appellee, v. UNITED BLOOD SERVICES, Appellant.
Opinion filed December 19, 1996.

JUSTICE FREEMAN delivered the opinion of the court:

This case primarily concerns the standard of care under section 3 of the Blood and Organ Transaction Liability Act (Blood Shield Act) (Ill. Rev. Stat. 1983, ch. 111½, par. 5101 et seq.), against which the conduct of a nonprofit blood bank charged with negligence in collecting whole blood contaminated with the human immunodeficiency virus (HIV) must be measured.

Plaintiff, Marietta Advincula, as the special administrator of the estate of her husband, Ronaldo Advincula, deceased, brought wrongful death (Ill. Rev. Stat. 1983, ch. 70, par. 1 et seq.), family expense (Ill. Rev. Stat. 1983, ch. 40, par. 1015), and survival actions (Ill. Rev. Stat. 1983, ch. 110½, par. 27--6) in the circuit court of Cook County against defendant, United Blood Services (UBS). UBS operates nonprofit blood banks which collect donated whole human blood and is an operating division of Blood Systems, Inc., a nonprofit Arizona corporation.

Following trial, the jury returned a verdict of $2.14 million in plaintiff's favor on all claims. UBS filed a post-trial motion for judgment notwithstanding the verdict or, alternatively, a new trial. The trial court denied the motion, and defendant appealed.

A sharply divided appellate panel affirmed, issuing three separate published opinions: the majority opinion delivered by Justice Scariano, a special concurrence by Justice DiVito, urging remand for retrial, and a dissent by Justice McCormick. 274 Ill. App. 3d 573. These published opinions addressed the appropriate standard of care under section 3 of the Act and proper application of the standard. A Supreme Court Rule 23 order (134 Ill. 2d R. 23) addressed remaining issues, e.g., proof of proximate cause, admissibility of expert opinion testimony and time-barring of the survival action.

Following the decision, the appellate court issued a certificate of importance pursuant to Supreme Court Rule 316 (134 Ill. 2d R. 316) and article VI, section 4(c), of the Illinois Constitution of 1970 (Ill. Const. 1970, art. VI, □4(c)). We assumed jurisdiction and granted the American National Red Cross, the American Association of Blood Banks (AABB), the American Blood Resources Association (ABRA) and Abbott Laboratories permission to file amicus curiae briefs in support of UBS. We granted similar permission to the Illinois Trial Lawyers Association and the Association of Trial Lawyers of America, which support plaintiff. 134 Ill. 2d R. 345. The thrust of the amici curiae support concerns the interpretation of section 3 with respect to standard of care.

Plaintiff initially moved unsuccessfully to dismiss the appeal, contesting jurisdiction. Plaintiff states that she incorporates that motion in her brief and requests its reconsideration. Such request in this form is not properly before the court. See Ill. Rev. Stat. 1983, ch. 110, par. 2--620; 134 Ill.

Author's aside: *It is ironic that Mr. Advincula and my mother were both treated for heart problems. Coincidentally, two days prior to this opinion, a consent decree ordering a blood recall was filed in federal court, with the New York Blood Center as the defendant. United Blood Services (UBS) contracted the New York Blood Center to test its blood. UBS, owned by Blood System Inc., supplied blood to thousands in the Chicagoland area. The consent decree cited numerous problems and deficiencies in the standards of this blood banking facility. The contract to do the testing at the New York Blood Center came about after the FDA threatened to cancel UBS's license. The revocation was due to the numerous violations found in 1994 at their Chicago location.*

Chapter 6

January 14, 1997

Document from FDA to NYBC
RE: Consent Decree Correspondence

"Appropriate follow-up, i.e. recall, should be conducted on blood products from donors for which samples cannot be obtained for retesting" (page 2 of two, numbers 4 and 5).

"Lookback should be initiated for donors to have confirmed reactive viral marker tests results."

Document dated 1997 (FDA-OCI)
Sealed Complaint-Office of Criminal Investigations

From in or about 1993 up to and including in or about November 1996, in the Southern District of New York, Eliazar "Joey" Maniago, the defendant—unlawfully, willfully, knowingly, and with intent to defraud and mislead—did introduce and deliver for introduction into interstate commerce a drug, to wit, blood, that was adulterated, to wit, the defendant adulterated blood to be tested for viruses such as HIV and hepatitis by willfully manipulating the methods used in, and the facilities and controls used for the manufacturing, processing, and packaging of blood and blood products. The FDA, OCI, and FBI completed the investigation (page 1).

E. SLAUGHTER SR.

U.S. FOOD AND DRUG ADMINISTRATION
NEW YORK DISTRICT
850 Third Avenue, BROOKLYN, NEW YORK 11232

Telephone: [718] 965-5300 ext. 5301

**CERTIFIED MAIL
RETURN RECEIPT REQUESTED**
January 14, 1997

Ms. Jenni Lee Robins
Responsible Head
New York Blood Center, Inc.
310 East 67th Street
New York, NY 10021

RE: CONSENT DECREE CORRESPONDENCE

Dear Ms. Robins:

The Food and Drug Administration (FDA) has reviewed New York Blood Center, Inc.'s (NYBC) letter dated December 27, 1996 with attachments which you forwarded in response to FDA's December 20, 1996, letter requesting that retention samples be retested and requesting a listing of voided test runs. **FDA likewise has reviewed the December 27, 1996 report which NYBC submitted pursuant to paragraph N.C.I (Testing of Blood Products) of the Consent Decree of Permanent Injunction entered on December 17, 1996 in the case United States v. New York Blood Center, et. al., 96 Civ 9464 (RPP)(SDNY)("Consent Decree").**

FDA notes that your December 27, 1996 letter and the accompanying attachments do not adequately address FDA's questions relative to viral marker testing performed by NYBC. While NYBC's analysis of the incidence rates before and after monitoring began suggests that the rates are consistent with published studies, your analysis lacks the power to detect the types of improper test procedure/result modifications that have been alleged to have occurred at NYBC. **Accordingly, in order to accurately identify those discrete blood products that may have been improperly released, retesting of the products (retention samples) or the donors would be necessary. Your response indicates that current retention samples are unsuitable for retesting. FDA advises, therefore, that NYBC begin taking the following steps immediately:**

1. **All extant blood products, including distributed products, manufactured from blood tested for viral markers between September 1, 1991 and November 20, 1996 should be quarantined.**

2. Extant blood products from donors with non-reactive test results obtained subsequent to November 20, 1996 may be released from quarantine.

3. **All donors tested for viral markers between September, 1991 and November 20, 1996 should be contacted and retested if non-reactive test results have not been obtained subsequent to November 20, 1996.**

New York Blood Center, Inc.
Page 2

4. **Appropriate follow up, i.e. recall, should be conducted on blood products from donors for which samples cannot be obtained for retesting.**

5. **Lookback should be initiated for donors found to have confirmed reactive viral marker test results.**

    FDA has the following comments relative to your December 27, 1996 report submitted pursuant to paragraph IV.C.I of the Decree.

1. The report does not indicate whether NYBC has conducted an internal investigation into the allegations of improper viral marker testing practices at NYBC. If an investigation has been conducted, please describe the details of the investigation and what corrective action(s) NYBC will institute as a result of its investigation.

2. The report does not explain the details of the viral marker testing monitoring program. Please provide specifics about the ongoing monitoring program and describe the data that NYBC will analyze to determine the effectiveness of the program. Also, please indicate how long NYBC intends the monitoring program to remain in place and the rationale for this decision.

3. FDA is unclear as to why NYBC included standard operating procedures (SOPS) with the report. Please indicate whether NYBC plans an assessment of the SOPS to assure that procedures meet the conditions set forth in section IV.C of the Consent Decree or whether the SOPS currently meet the conditions set forth in the Consent Decree. Please note that NYBC has the responsibility to ensure that its SOPS comply with the Consent Decree, laws, and applicable regulations. FDA will review SOPS during subsequent inspections of your firm,

    FDA requests that you respond to the above questions within 10 days of receipt of this letter. As with other correspondence submitted under the Consent Decree, the response should be prominently marked "NYBC Consent Decree Correspondence" and be sent to the District Director, New York District Office, 850 3rd Avenue, Brooklyn, NY, 11232, with a copy to the Director, Center for Biologics Evaluation and Research, HFM-1, 1401 Rockville Pike, Suite 200N, Rockville, MD 20852-1448.

    FDA agrees to the meeting requested by your firm. The meeting has been scheduled to be held in Bethesda (National Institutes of Health, Building 29B, conference room B, 1-3pm) on January 15, 1997 to address any questions concerning this correspondence. If you have any other issues you would like to discuss at the meeting, please forward them to FDA, in writing, by 5 p.m., Tuesday, January 14, 1997.

Sincerely,

Acting District Director

Author's aside: *This correspondence was a response to an NYBC letter dated December 27, 1996. "NYBC analysis lacks the power to detect the types of improper test procedure/result modifications that have been alleged to have occurred at NYBC" (page 1, paragraph 2).*

January 31, 1997

Mom admitted to South Suburban Hospital.

February 2, 1997

Mom diagnosed with leukopenia and granulomatosis. "Wegener's" was handwritten next to "granulomatosis." The medical report also stated Mom had a normal heartbeat.

February 10, 1997

Document from FDA to NYBC, Ms. Jenni Lee Robins

Subject: NYBC Consent Decree Correspondence

As you know, FDA's January 14 letter advised that NYBC should begin taking immediate steps to quarantine certain extent (in-date existing) blood products, retest identified donors (paragraph 1, page 1 of four pages).

Because of the serious nature of the improper testing, FDA has no assurance that the blood samples tested from September 1, 1991, through November 20, 1996, were properly tested. See declaration of Curtis L. Scribner, MD, a copy of which is enclosed herewith (page 2, paragraph 1).

THE AMERICAN GENOCIDE

U.S. FOOD AND DRUG ADMINISTRATION
NEW YORK DISTRICT
850 Third Avenue, BROOKLYN, NEW YORK 11232

Telephone: [718] 965-5300 ext. 5301

NYBC CONSENT DECREE CORRESPONDENCE

BY FACSIMILE
And
CERTIFIED MAIL
RETURN RECEIPT REQUESTED

February 10, 1997

Ms. Jenni Lee Robins
Responsible Head
New York Blood Center, Inc.
310 East 67th Street
New York, NY 10021

RE: UNITED STATES V. NEW YORK BLOOD CENTER, INC.,
et al., 96 Civ. 9464 RPP (S.D.N.Y.)

Dear Ms. Robins:

The Food and Drug Administration (FDA) has reviewed New York Blood Center, Inc.'s (NYBC) letter dated January 22, 1997, with attachments, which responds to FDA's January 14, 1997 letter. As you know, FDA's January 14 letter advised that NYBC should begin taking immediate steps to quarantine certain extant (in-date existing) blood products, retest identified donors, follow-up on blood products collected from donors for which samples could not be obtained and viral marker retesting could not be performed, and initiate lookback, as appropriate.

The proposals described in NYBC's January 22, 1997 letter and the accompanying attachments are not sufficient to accomplish FDA's goal of minimizing the potential risk to the public health posed by the extant blood products.

Specifically, FDA was advised by certain laboratory technicians employed at NYBC that certain other technicians improperly and fraudulently tested blood samples for viral markers. Following an internal investigation of the testing irregularities NYBC management entered into Consent Decree. These irregularities included failure to follow manufacturer's instructions for testing blood products after obtaining invalid test results for a plate and/or tray of blood samples, in that NYBC personnel adjusted the controls, records, procedures, and or equipment to obtain test results that appeared valid, an d NYBC personnel failed to retain and/or eliminated test

New York Blood Center, Inc.
Page 2

records. **Because of the serious nature of the improper testing, FDA has no assurance that the blood samples tested from September 1, 1991 through November 20, 1996 were properly tested. See Declaration of Curtis L. Scribner, M.D., a copy of which is enclosed herewith.**

NYBC has suggested that because its incidence rate analysis of invalid test runs before and after monitoring of the testing began in November 1996 shows that the viral marker rate is consistent with incidence rates in published studies, FDA can be assured that if manipulation of testing occurred, it had no effect on the validity of the testing. FDA disagrees. NYBC's analysis does not answer the question of which plates were manipulated, and therefore not properly tested for viral markers. Accordingly, FDA believes NYBC must quarantine the extant units and retest the blood or the donors.

In its January 22, 1997 response, NYBC has objected to FDA's notification of quarantine and retesting on the theory that there are very few units of extant products and some may not be available for testing. Likewise, NYBC argues that there does not appear to be a sufficiently large source of blood components to be retested to yield results of appropriate power or sensitivity to rate the magnitude of any potential risk. Both of these arguments miss the point.

The fact that the amount of extant blood products is small is irrelevant to the issue of whether they were properly tested. Moreover, the fact that there are a small number of units remaining will make it less onerous for NYBC to quarantine and retest them. Second, regardless of whether retesting will yield results of appropriate power or sensitivity, retesting will assure the safety of the blood products before they are used by consumers. Your letter does not explain why some of the units may be unavailable for testing. However, the unavailability of some units provides no basis for not assuring the safety of units that are available. If it is true that some units can not be tested, these units--which were tested under stunningly inadequate conditions--should be destroyed. Please identify all such units and provide an inventory to FDA by February 28, 1997. As NYBC acknowledges, the extant blood products continue to be used. Therefore, NYBC's proposal of studying the seroconversion rates among the rapidly growing group or population of post November 20, 1996 repeat donors as the only risk assessment study is not adequate. In the three months that NYBC estimates it will take to have sufficient data to detect a relative increase in any viral marker, all of the extant product may have been used. For this reason, FDA has requested that NYBC take steps to quarantine the extant blood products.

Because that portion of FDA's January 14, 1997 letter addressing extant products was forwarded to NYBC pursuant to Paragraph VI.A. of the Consent Decree, and NYBC's response dated January 22, 1997, was forwarded to the New York District Office and the Center for Biologics Evaluation and Research (CBER) pursuant to Paragraph VI.B., after review of NYBC's response by the District and CBER, FDA hereby affirms and modifies its January 14, 1997 notification and notifies NYBC that it must begin taking the following steps immediately:

1. Quarantine the estimated ----------------units of extant blood products specified on page 4 of your January 22, 1997 letter, manufactured from blood tested for viral markers

Author's aside: It is important to note that FDA records indicate the problem existed from September 1, 1991, through November 20, 1996. The newspaper account stated 1994 to 1996.

March 24, 1997

I visited Mom at South Suburban Hospital. While there, she stated, "I am going home tomorrow. The doctors said I would if I continued to eat well."

March 25, 1997

Mom died at South Suburban Hospital. Her death certificate did not indicate Wegener's granulomatosis as cause of death. Dr. Rao, from Columbus Hospital, signed off on her death certificate.

March 29, 1997

Mom's funeral was held at Midwest Memorial Chapel. She had a great home-going.

April 1997

I received a letter of acceptance into Cooley School of Law.

July 1997

My daughter underwent back surgery at UIC Hospital. I was amazed when doctors said she had to give her own blood for the surgery. This was new to me. I believe it was done this way because their blood supply was tainted.

July 4, 1997

"New York Blood Center's Head Resigns"—Dr. Adamson

AOL News, July 4, 1997

The center distributes blood to 250 hospitals, covering twenty million people. In a typical year, about seven hundred thousand units are checked. Government officials said there is no evidence that public health is threatened.

Author's aside: *This appears to be a contradiction of their findings and the consent decree correspondences. The year 1997 was one of the worst years of my life because many relatives died: my cousin Larry at UIC; my ninety-four-year-old great-aunt, Mrs. Barnes, after whom Mom was named, died in July; cousin Bobbie Jean in August; my mother's half-sister, Annie Lee, in September; not to mention her friend and cousin, Ruth, in July 1996.*

There were many other funerals that year, including coworkers; I believe some may have been infected by the blood supply. With so many deaths occurring, I felt that something terribly wrong was happening at the hospitals. The number of friends and relatives to die during the recall and announcement period were many; after the recall was announced in December of 1998, the number of deaths dropped dramatically.

THE AMERICAN GENOCIDE

July 14, 1997

Subject: Recall—Urgent

Subject-Recall-Urgent

A New York Blood Center

310 E, 67th Street, New York, NY 10021
211/570-3000 Fax 212/570-3195

July 14, 1997

RECALL URGENT

Dear Dr-

We are notifying you of a recall of identified blood components (red blood cells, platelets, cryoprecipiate, and fresh frozen plasma). **This recall is an extension of the NYBC February 13, 1997 quarantine notice and is based on additional information. This recall is being conducted due to our inability to assure that these products were properly tested for the vial markers anti-HCV, anti-HBC and HTV p24 antigen (see Attachment 1).**

The relevant component(s) listed by viral marker that were shipped to your facility are identified on the attached form. Please complete rte form(s), documenting the disposition of these units, and return the completed form(s) by fax or rail no later than August 15, 1997. Note: In NYBC's quarantine notice of February 13, 1997 any extant (in-date) blood components in inventory as of November 20, 1996 were to be discarded. If any extant components exist, please discard immediately and note date of discard in the disposition column.

If a patient were transfused with any transfusable component noted on the attached anti-HCV recall list, we recommend that you notify the attending physician of this transfusion event. If deemed appropriate by the attending physician, we recommend the patient be notified. If you wish to have the patient tested, the form, for blood sample submission to the New York Blood Center is also enclosed. This testing is free of charge.

If a patient were transfused with any of the transfusable components noted on the attached HIV p24 or anti-HBC recall lists, we recommend that you notify the attending physician of this transfusion event.

This recall is being conducted voluntarily by NYBC with the full knowledge of the U.S. Food and Drug Administration and the New York State Department of Health. We greatly appreciate your cooperation. Physicians should contact Dr. Celso Bianco, Vice President, Medical Affairs, at (212) 570-3101 to discuss related medical issues. For all other questions, please contact Debra Kessler, Director of Regional Services, at (212) 570-3021.

Sincerely,

Thomas F. Zuck, MD
Responsible Head and
Interim Chief Operating Officer

Author's aside: This letter is an extension of the February 13, 1997, recall letter from NYBC to its providers.

Subject: Recall—Urgent

The blood suppliers, hospitals, their agents, etc. were advised repeatedly by NYBC to retest donors and advise recipients if they received tainted blood products. Mom should have been notified on or before February 13, 1997, more than a month before her death, according to a document dated July 14, 1997, and the consent decree dated December 17, 1996.

I believed that from November 1996 until her death, Columbus Hospital, South Shore Hospital, and her attending doctors were aware of the cause of her illness and death, and they not only kept it a secret from our family but suppressed the truth when they told us she was suffering from Wegener's granulomatosis. They treated her with medication for Wegener's granulomatosis, which is also prescribed to patients with hepatitis and leukemia. Although her symptoms were consistent with Wegener's granulomatosis, it is hard to believe Mom had that disease because it is very rare in African-Americans. Something told me it wasn't what they were saying it was.

An October 15, 1998, Illinois Department of Public Health letter acknowledges receiving complaints about South Suburban Hospital. I filed my complaint because I felt something was wrong and hoped I would uncover facts and clues about Mom's death.

Chapter 7

December 2, 1998

I had a dream something important would appear in the newspaper. I woke in the middle of the night and observed a beautiful full moon. This was when the dreams and hunches kicked in and never stopped. I remember a similar dream from years ago. On October 20, 1979, I was living in New Jersey, and I dreamed about my sister's death the day she was murdered in Chicago. I eventually tracked down and met her killer, who beat the case on a technicality and was found guilty of a lesser charge. But because of my deep-seated belief in my faith, I did not seek revenge for her death, and he never knew who I was.

December 2, 1998

Chicago Tribune

"Years later, 40,000 warned of possible transfusion risk."

Years later, 40,000 warned of possible transfusion risk

By Jeremy Manier
TRIBUNE STAFF WRITER

In an unusual move more than two years after concern first arose, a New York blood bank is notifying some 40,000 Chicago-area residents who received transfusions from 1994 to 1996 that they may be at risk—however remote—for viral infections such as hepatitis and HIV.

Officials at the New York Blood Center, the largest independent blood-products company in the country, say inadequate controls on screening tests may have left open the possibility that tainted blood was passed on to as many as 28 hospitals in Chicago, including major centers such as Northwestern Memorial Hospital and the University of Chicago Hospitals.

No cases of infection have been linked to the blood, and federal and blood-bank officials say they have had to carefully balance the risk of alarming recipients with the need to inform the public.

"For the most part, people just need some reassurance," said Dr. Robert Jones, president and CEO of the New York center. "It may seem like overkill, but we're trying to be very conservative about this."

A public-health announcement in local newspapers Tuesday and

SEE BLOOD, PAGE 20

December 2, 1998

Chicago Sun-Times

"Warning issued on donor blood."

An FDA spokeswoman was quoted as stating, "Based on what we know, we believe the risk to be very low."

"Two employees at NYBC were convicted of conspiracy and falsifying

THE AMERICAN GENOCIDE

statements to the FDA. Several other cities were also affected according to this report. They were New York, Memphis, and Pittsburgh. Chicago alone had 150,000 units formed for screening to NYBC from United Blood Services, also known as UBS."

Warning issued on donor blood

By BRYAN SMITH
STAFF REPORTER

Thousands of Chicago area patients may have received blood that was improperly screened for diseases such as AIDS and hepatitis, officials said Tuesday.

Officials at a New York blood bank said that as many as 35,000 patients who received transfusions in 28 Chicago area hospitals between June, 1994, and December, 1996, may have received the improperly tested blood.

The testing problems were attributed to two employees taking improper shortcuts. The two

were criminally prosecuted and convicted. Blood experts said chances that anyone contracted a transfusion-transmitted infection were remote because of multiple testing guards.

"We're really acting conservatively."

Turn to next p

Author's aside: In the Chicagoland area, twenty-eight hospitals were affected, including South Shore, Columbus, UIC, where my cousin died, and another hospital, Little Company of Mary, where my aunt passed away. Some individuals actually received a blood transfusion during this recall. While many died or received blood after November 19, 1996, numerous labels had duplicate donors; and FDA records stated, "NYBC lacked the power to detect the types of improper test procedure/result." This could have allowed the adulterated blood supply into the hospitals.

December 2, 1998

I contacted NYBC and was referred to South Shore Hospital. I also made contact with LifeSource attorney, Richard Birdell Jr.

December 3, 1998

I called FDA spokeswoman, Lenore Gelb.

December 3, 1998

I called Columbus Hospital. Dan McCarthy said, "I will look into it."

December 3, 1998

I contacted FDA Biological Research and tried to reach the president of New York Blood Center, Robert L. Jones. His secretary referred me to Ms. Kessler, who told me I didn't have a case.

December 3, 1998

I called South Shore Hospital and spoke with a doctor, who said he would meet with Drs. Dayon and Tyson in an attempt to trace donors to see if they were healthy.

December 3, 1998

FDA representative Jane Hardy returned my call. Dr. Shapiro of LifeSource called and stated that she couldn't help me.

December 9, 1998

I began to contact numerous attorneys by phone and in writing. I began visiting the Harold Washington Library to research legal and medical citations concerning the blood recall. While I researched documents, something often happened to help me along. Usually, the day before I planned a trip to the library, perhaps while sleeping, a clue would pop into my head, leading me to relevant information concerning the blood recall and the effects on Mary and the other victims.

February 12, 1999

Letter addressed to FDA for documents concerning blood-screening flaw—New York Blood Center (1994–1996).

February 26, 1999

Freedom of Information Act (FOIA) request I sent a letter to Columbus Hospital requesting information about Mom's diagnosis and infection.

February 26, 1999

I received a letter from the FDA requesting a fee for FOIA information.

March 7, 1999

I sent a letter to attorney R. Charrow in an attempt to retain his services. In answer, he requested medical records from South Shore and Columbus hospitals.

March 23, 1999

I filed a pro se complaint in federal court with these specifics:

Slaughter v. New York Blood Center, President John Adamson;
Blood System Inc., President Daniel O'Connor;
United Blood Services of Chicago, LifeSource of Glenview, President William Patman;
South Shore Hospital, President Jesus Ong, Dr. C. Tyson, Dr. D. Dayon;
Columbus Hospital, President Theresa Peck, Dr. Hedgers;
All defendants individually and in their official capacities.

Requested class action status:

Count 1 - $5,000,000 compensatory and $5,000,000 punitive

Count 2 - $15,000,000 compensatory and $15,000,000 punitive

For injunctive and other relief:

I had to file my complaint and represent myself because there wasn't enough time to find a lawyer. I researched the law and filed before the statute of limitations expired. All defendants were served. I received a couple of phone calls from attorneys after they received their summonses, asking for more time to respond. They thought I was an attorney. After the lawsuit was filed, it was time to get a medical evaluation for the courts and continue my search for an attorney.

As I said before, several attorneys told me they were impressed with my research; some were amazed at how well I articulated my lawsuit.

After the summonses were served, I was surprised to observe what appeared to be surveillance on my house and myself. It could only have been an opposing defendant attempting to find out who I was and what I was up to, and I never thought my family was in danger. There was no paranoia about this surveillance or any other matter in this story. Soon afterward, the surveillance ceased.

April 1999

Mr. Harper, of South Shore Hospital, offered to settle; but he wanted an attorney involved. He never gave a price, nor did he put it in writing.

I was still finding it difficult to secure an attorney, and I eventually ended up with Mr. Jordan. I informed him of Mr. Harper's settlement offer. I was also able to obtain a certificate of merit from Dr. Bruce ——. His certificate stated, among other things, "I am of the opinion, which I hold to a reasonable degree of medical certainty, that the actions of the defendants caused or contributed to the chain of events which ultimately led to Mary's sepsis and death."

He named the following defendants in this certificate: Dr. Tyson, Dr. Dayon, Columbus-Cabrini Health Systems, South Shore Hospital, New York Blood Center, Blood System Inc., United Blood Services of Chicago, and LifeSource of Glenview. Some violations were for applicable standards of care, deviations from standards of care, failure to properly screen the transfusion specimen, and failure to establish/enforce safety protocol.

In addition to this certificate of merit, Karen ——, a nurse with a graduate degree and extensive nursing and teaching experience, stated in her laboratory studies of Mom's symptoms, "After receiving the blood transfusions, there was evidence of infection/inflammation or some reaction. The renal insufficiency rapidly worsened, resulting in the need for hemodialysis. There were no laboratory studies for hepatitis" (April 1999).

E. SLAUGHTER SR.

Certificate of Merit

I am a physician and surgeon licensed to practice medicine in all of its branches. I have reviewed the medical records, facts, representations of Lt. E. Slaughter, Complaint in The United States District Court, 99 C 1888, US-FDA Consent Decree, 1997, by and between the U.S. and New York Blood Center, Inc. and other relevant material of the attached matter and find that there is a reasonable and meritorious basis for a health care malpractice lawsuit. I am knowledgeable in the relevant issues, qualified by experience and training and I have practiced in the area in question within the past six years. For the reasons to follow below, I am of the opinion, which I hold to a reasonable degree of medical certainty, that the actions of the defendants, reasonably caused or contributed to the chain of events which ultimately led to Willie Slaughter's sepsis and death.

In September, 1996 C. TYSON, M.D., violated the applicable standard of care when he caused a blood transfusion to occur on decedent where her blood indices did not mandate such a procedure. Decedent contracted a septic condition of the blood as a direct result of the improper transfusion.

In September, 1996 D.DAYON, M.D., violated the applicable standard of care when he caused a blood transfusion to occur on decedent where her blood indices did not mandate such a procedure. Decedent contracted a septic condition of the blood as a direct result of the improper transfusion.

Columbus-Cabrini Health Systems deviated from the standard of care in its failure to timely diagnose and/or treat sepsis.

SOUTH SHORE HOSPITAL failed to establish/enforce proper and safe protocols for the use of transfusions and failed to take appropriate measures to screen for the use of non-infected blood.

New York Blood Center negligently failed to screen the transfusion specimen and failed to put in place measures designed to catch such contamination.

Blood System, Inc. negligently failed to screen the transfusion specimen and failed to put in place measures designed to catch such contamination.

United Blood Services of Chicago negligently failed to screen the transfusion specimen and failed to put in place measures designed to catch such contamination.

Lifesource of Glenview negligently failed to screen the transfusion specimen and failed to put in place measures designed to catch such contamination.

Respectfully,

A licensed physician.

• Page 2   April 29, 1999

ANA on 10-23-96 was positive (this can indicate connective tissue disease like lupus or rheumatoid arthritis). The serum potassium became critically elevated on 10-24-96 indicating worsening kidney disease and/or failure. I assume hemodialysis was started at this time.

A chest x-ray showed an enlarged heart which could be related to the renal failure. The kidney biopsy 10-31-96 clinically demonstrated glomerulonephritis, kidney disease leading to kidney failure.

Blood cultures in January, 1997 showed the presence of organisms in the blood - possibly related to the Quinton catheter.

After receiving the blood transfusions, there was evidence of infection/inflammation or some reaction. The renal insufficiency rapidly worsened, resulting in the need for hemodialysis.

There were no laboratory studies for hepatitis.

Please advise if I can further assist you in this matter.

Karen

Ironically, the infections that caused Mom's renal failure may have been consistent with Wegener's granulomatosis; but according to two medical evaluations, the renal failure appeared to have been caused by tainted blood transfusions. Even if she had Wegener's granulomatosis, according to the medical evaluations, Wegener's granulomatosis wasn't present prior to the blood transfusion. Why didn't Dr. Rao indicate Wegener's granulomatosis as the cause of death on her death certificate? They stated her illness was Wegener's granulomatosis, an acute nephritic syndrome; but her symptoms were also consistent with acute viral infections such as HBV, EBV, HZV, hepatitis, and staphylococcal infections.

May 1999

I had a dream that Mr. Jordan dismissed a real estate case he was hired to prosecute. When I doubted the truth of the dream, a calendar fell off the wall as if something were trying to alert me. A few days later, I went downtown to see if the dream was true. After retrieving the court document for the real estate deal, I learned he had dismissed the case on August 5, 1998. I was stunned. As I returned home, many things crossed my mind, but then I realized that whatever had alerted me to Jordan's misrepresentation most likely had been assisting me for a while. For example, I usually dreamed the day before about what to look up in the library. I had thought it was normal; but I now realize that throughout all of this, even before Mom's death, I had been given hints, such as the hunch to go and see her before she died. Something has, in some way, been in contact with me.

May 12, 1999

Attending court this day, I seriously considered terminating Mr. Jordan's services on the spot. When the court clerk announced *Slaughter v. New York Blood Center et al.*, I was amazed at the number of opposing attorneys. I had an attorney I no longer trusted, and I felt lost and defeated. After an opposing attorney attempted to intimidate me, I asked the Lord for help. The judge set a status hearing for June 16, 1999. Leaving court, I observed Mr. Jordan talking with a few of the defendants' attorneys.

Following that court date, I began looking for another attorney. I knew, after verifying the dream about the property case dismissal that a new attorney was urgently needed.

May 13, 1999

I contacted the United States Attorney's Office. I reached assistant United States attorney Deborah Y. Yeoh of New York. I informed her of the court status, the delay of notification, and the defendant's refusal to investigate my mother's transfusions. I was surprised to be able to pick up the phone, talk to an assistant United States attorney, and have a pleasant conversation. I continued to receive letters from attorneys I had previously contacted.

May 17, 1999

A deal was signed with Dr. Bruce —— to arrange for expert witnesses.

May 20, 1999

I received a letter from Mr. Larry ——, from a prominent law office, which stated that his office would be unable to assist me. These letters were not discouraging, but they delayed my termination of Mr. Jordan. I thought I could use him for advice if needed but knew he couldn't be trusted in court.

June 2, 1999

It became obvious to Mr. Jordan that his services were not going to be needed in the future.

As I conversed with other attorneys, I became more and more frustrated. Most wanted an autopsy, but we never had one done.

June 15, 1999

The judge sent out notices that he was dismissing the case for lack of jurisdiction. I had one year to refile my complaint in Cook County court. We did not have to appear in federal court on June 16, 1999. The judge also stated, "After this opinion had been completed and was awaiting final transcription, Mr. Jordan served notice that he had proposed to appear at the scheduled June 16th status hearing to ask, to leave, to withdraw because of substantial and overwhelming differences [that] have arisen between counsel and his client, Mr. Slaughter." The opinion rendered any such motion moot.

July 14, 1999

I filed a complaint with the Attorney Registration and Disciplinary Commission requesting an investigation of Mr. Jordan's actions.

August 3, 1999

The commission launched its investigation.

August 12, 1999

Mr. Robert — hired me to investigate an asbestos claim against a local college. He also agreed to take over my case.

August 16, 1999

The federal judge entered another opinion. Mr. Jordan filed a motion to have the language changed in the prior motion to say he was retained, not appointed, by the court. The judge replied, "As stated earlier, what has been said in this memorandum does not affect the opinion's substantive ruling in the opinion, nor does it affect the determination that Mr. Jordan's motion for leave to withdraw was rendered moot by dismissal of the case."

August 30, 1999

An agreement with Mr. Robert — to take over the case was signed.

October 1, 1999

The commission concluded their investigation on Mr. Jordan. They stated, "We have concluded our inquiry into the above matter and have determined that there is not a sufficient basis for further action by this office." Although I offered a voice mail recording of Mr. Jordan saying, "we will be going to trial soon" and giving updates on the case, he had convinced the commission to believe him.

December 8, 1999

The vice president of Blood Systems Inc. asked for medical records to resolve the claim, but any discussion about the claim had to go through my attorney.

May 19, 2000

I received a letter from Blood Systems Inc. which said, in part, "Dear Mr. Slaughter: It is unfortunate that we are unable to reach agreement on resolving this matter, and I remain open to further discussions." This letter was written after I informed Blood Systems Inc. that I was no longer working with Mr. Robert — and had rejected their first offer.

May 26, 2000

I submitted a letter to Johnny Cochran's law firm, addressed to Mr. Randall. I enclosed medical records, medical evaluations, and letters from Blood Systems Inc. in which they attempted to settle the case. The firm later replied, stating they could not take the case because there was not enough time to investigate and prepare.

June 13, 2000

Another letter from Blood Systems Inc. was delivered. In it, they stated, "In return for this settlement, Blood Systems will pay you the amount of ten thousand dollars ($10,000) upon reaching agreement on the terms and conditions of a settlement agreement. If you want to proceed with a settlement under these terms, please let me know. I will prepare a settlement agreement for your review."

June 14, 2000

I refiled the blood transfusion case in the Circuit Court of Cook County.

July 20, 2000

A complaint was sent to FDA representative Donna Shalala.

July 21, 2000

A complaint was sent to Director John R. Lumpkin, MD, of the Illinois Department of Public Health. In summary, several hospitals, but mainly South Shore, are my concern. For many years, thousands of patients received blood transfusions at these hospitals with adulterated blood products. The FDA's consent decree states this occurred from 1991 to November 20, 1996, at least. The consent decree was signed in December 1996. A class I recall was part of this decree. Dr. C. Tyson, of South Shore Hospital, and Dr. Hedgers, of Columbus Hospital, were part of this complaint.

July 31, 2000

I received a letter from FDA.

Reference: Freedom of Information Act Request Received records concerning United Blood Services

August 4, 2000

I received a letter from the Illinois Department of Public Health Deputy Director, William A. Bell. "We are referring a copy of your letter to the Illinois Department of Professional Regulation. The Department of Professional Regulation licenses, investigates, and disciplines physicians in Illinois." This was in response to my letter dated July 21, 2000, complaining about Dr. C. Tyson and Dr. Hedgers. I also filed complaints via the Internet.

August 24, 2000

I received another letter from the FDA, acknowledging the receipt of my request for additional information. I requested information that had been deleted by the FDA.

October 2000

My uncle RJ said something to me that rekindled the spiritual moments of which I have spoken several times in this story. On his deathbed, he stated, "I am ready to die to be with my sister." He was speaking of my mom. He had an amazing smile on his face, similar to the one he wore at his funeral. He died a day or two after making that comment.

February 12, 2001

There came a letter from the FDA, stating that they were having difficulties processing my request for the deleted information. I was referred to Robert Stevenson of Access Litigation.

February 15, 2001

I faxed the FOIA request for the deleted information to the FDA's representative, Robert Stevenson.

February 26, 2001

The letter from Robert Stevenson in part said, "If, however, you desire to review the deleted material, please make an additional request to the following address: FDA, Rockville, MD."

It was obvious, after ten months, that the FDA was giving me the runaround and would not release the deleted information.

March 4, 2001

Another request was faxed to Robert Stevenson.

March 8, 2001

Letter received from the FDA, which acknowledged receiving my request for the deleted records.

March 19, 2001

I wrote a letter to the Illinois Department of Public Health, requesting the status of my complaint against South Shore Hospital.

E. SLAUGHTER SR.

April 9, 2001

Letter from the Illinois Department of Public Health, RE: Illinois Freedom of Information Act request: "Dear Mr. Slaughter: A review of your complaint has determined that it should be investigated under the Illinois Hospital Licensing Act (210 ILCS85)." Related to South Shore Hospital and complaint.

Illinois Department of Public Health

George H. Ryan, Governor • John R. Lumpkin, M.D., M.P.H., Director

525-535 West Jefferson Street • Springfield, Illinois 62761-0001

April 9, 2001

RE: Illinois Freedom of Information Act request No. 01040571

Dear Mr. Slaughter:

This letter is in response to your Illinois Freedom of Information Act (FOIA) request addressed to John R. Lumpkin, M.D., M.P.H., Director, for a request received by the Department on 3/19/2001, for information related to South Shore Hospital and complaint number 00-2448.

A review of your complaint has determined that it should be investigated under the Illinois Hospital Licensing Act [210 ILCS85]. The complaint remains in our "open" file at this time. Hospital complaints are investigated based on the seriousness of the complaint and staff workload.

If you have any further questions, please contact Mr. Enrique J. Unanue at 217-782-7412, or in writing at the Illinois Department of Public Health, Division of Health Care Facilities and Programs, 525 W. Jefferson, 4th Floor, Springfield, IL 62761-0001. The Division's fax number is 217-782-0382. The Department's TTY, (for hearing impaired only), number is 800-547-0466.

Sincerely,

Brent M. DeMichael
Freedom of Information Officer

April 24, 2001

Letter from the FDA came, which denied another request for the deleted FOIA material. The reason for denial: "Trade secrets and confidential commercial information." This information was first requested on May 6, 2000. The deleted information appeared to give the approximate number of units of blood collected by UBS under contract, how many Chicagoland hospitals it supplied, and the screening tests completed on the approximate number of "donor packs" per month. A potential duplicate donors report and other records for irradiation by contractors were incomplete. No written contracts or reports of defective materials existed. How could these be trade secrets or confidential? This was an appeal for previously denied/deleted information.

May 2001

Mr. Geoffrey — was hired, on a contingency basis, to prosecute and/or settle claim with the parties involved.

Mr. Geoffrey — attempted to renegotiate a settlement with Blood System Inc. without keeping me informed of the details. There was very poor communication between us; at times, it took him over two weeks to return a phone call.

After I attempted to reach him several times, unsuccessfully, I fired him by fax. He responded to the fax on July 1, 2001, with an apology and explanation.

July 11, 2001

A letter was faxed to Blood Systems Inc. informing them that Mr. Geoffrey —'s service had been terminated.

August 29, 2001

State of New York Department of Health refused to process an FOIA request.

September 5, 2001

I received a letter from the Illinois Department of Professional Regulation in reference to Drs. Hedgers and Tyson. "The board has determined that no violation of the Medical Practice Act of 1987 has occurred in this matter and has ordered this filed closed. Please be informed that the file concerning these allegations is confidential and will not be made available for public inspection" (from Robert Kriz, chief of Medical Investigations).

February 28, 2002

Letter from the FDA, in reference to the appeal and Freedom of Information Act request: "We have already released certain materials to you and are denying the remainder of your request."

July 26, 2002

News headline, legal affairs reporter:

"The FBI is investigating into the unnamed 'go-between' who might have split the $30,000 with the 'sitting judge' who appointed Smith." Justice Freeman was questioned about this matter since it was he who appointed

Smith to the bench. During this investigation, Justice Freeman spoke at an engagement for an organization of which I am a member. I had the opportunity to speak to him and shake his hand. I felt bad about what the media was relaying in regard to him. I later wrote him a letter, offering my assistance, if he needed it. I recall that while researching the tainted blood cases, Justice Freeman's name appeared on the computer screen, detailing his opinion in the *Advincula* case. I was amazed at how this information came to me. I felt like an infinite intelligence was not only making me aware of the *Advincula* case, but was also giving me the opportunity to meet and greet Justice Freeman. My sympathetic feelings toward him eventually faded away.

Judge gets the maximum

July 26, 2002

BY ABDON M. PALLASCH LEGAL AFFAIRS REPORTER

A disgraced former Cook County judge got the maximum prison sentence of two years and three months in federal prison for a financial fraud conviction Thursday.

Though the conviction covered only financial fraud, prosecutors and even the judge in the case hinted there might be more to come as the investigation continues into whether George J.W. Smith paid a $30,000 bribe to get his seat on the bench.

"Though this case concludes here today, there is a certain pregnancy about this matter that will not come to an end today," U.S. District Judge Charles Norgle said.

Prosecutors said the investigation continues into the unnamed "go-between" who might have split the $30,000 with the "sitting judge" who appointed Smith.

Smith initially was appointed by State Supreme Court Justice Charles Freeman on a recommendation from former Ald. Edward Vrdolyak (10th). Freeman has denied receiving any money for the appointment, and Vrdolyak has declined comment.

The FBI pulled the files on 100 Cook County judges appointed in the past 10 years and interviewed all three state supreme court justices from Cook County--Freeman, Mary Ann McMorrow and the late Michael Bilandic-- about the process.

"The investigation continues," Assistant U.S. Attorney Dean Polales said.

Smith's lawyers told Norgle Thursday that Smith might be called before the grand jury.

"I heard it costs $30,000 to buy a judgeship in Cook County, but I didn't do it," Polales said Smith told FBI agents when they first confronted him.

Smith told agents the $20,000 he illegally withdrew in amounts small enough to evade federal detection was for concrete work on his house.

The agents visited the concrete worker Smith had referred them to 45 minutes after talking to Smith.

"As soon as they pulled up, Mr. Smith came out," Polales said. "He had instantly gone . . . to secure corroboration for the false stories."

Polales said four times Thursday that the $20,000 was "to pay a third party to influence a sitting judge to appoint him to the bench of the Circuit Court of Cook County."

Polales said Smith persuaded his then-wife to go along with the scheme "to conceal the fact that a payment was split between a go-between and the sitting judge."

Federal officials only learned of the scheme when the ex-wife was called in by the IRS to explain a discrepancy on the couple's tax form.

http://www.ipsn.org/judge_gets_the_maximum.htm

May 26, 2003

I sent a letter to the United States attorney of the Northern District of Illinois, asking to investigate my complaint. I forwarded my concerns to them because I believed the statute of limitations for prosecution was about to run out.

E. SLAUGHTER SR.

December 17, 2003

News headline:

Department of Justice

FOR IMMEDIATE RELEASE AG
WEDNESDAY, DECEMBER 17, 2003 (202) 514-2008
WWW.USDOJ.GOV TDD (202) 514-1888

FORMER ILLINOIS GOVERNOR RYAN INDICTED BY FEDERAL GRAND JURY

WASHINGTON, DC - U.S. Attorney General John Ashcroft and United States Attorney Patrick Fitzgerald of the Northern District of Illinois today announced that a federal grand jury in Chicago issued a 22-count superseding indictment against former Illinois Governor George H. Ryan, Sr., and businessman Lawrence E. Warner.

The indictment charges Ryan with racketeering conspiracy, mail fraud, and other crimes alleging public corruption, official misconduct, and fraudulent conduct during his terms as Illinois Secretary of State and Governor of Illinois.

Attorney General Ashcroft said, "On the stonewalls of the Justice Department in Washington are chiseled the words: 'No free government can survive that is not based on supremacy of the law.' When a public official abuses his office, he drains the reservoir of public trust on which our democratic institutions rely.

"In bringing these indictments, the Justice Department is seeking to protect the faith the American people must have in their government."

Ryan has been charged with a pattern of racketeering activity including: mail fraud; money laundering; extortion, attempted extortion, and extortion conspiracy; bribery; and obstruction of justice.

The indictment alleges that Ryan received illegal cash payments and gifts, vacations and personal services, and that members of his family received cash, loans, gifts and services totaling approximately $167,000. In addition, Ryan allegedly directed payments totaling more than $300,000 to Donald Udstuen, an associate and co-defendant. These transactions were allegedly concealed and disguised to prevent public exposure and possible criminal prosecution. In addition, the indictment alleges that Ryan repeatedly lied to federal agents about facts material to the investigation.

Ryan is charged with knowingly taking actions in his official capacity as Secretary of State to award state contracts to benefit the personal and financial interests of defendant Warner and certain other associates, while concealing, in violation of the law, his financial relationship with Warner and certain associates.

THE AMERICAN GENOCIDE

Former Governor George Ryan was indicted. The indictment alleged that George Ryan received illegal cash payments while he was the Illinois secretary of state. Ryan was quoted as saying that he knew there was a culture of corruption in the secretary of state's office. I had shaken his hand at a function a few months before his indictment, and I felt quite uncomfortable. It was a very strange feeling.

```
              UNITED STATES DISTRICT COURT
              NORTHERN DISTRICT OF ILLINOIS
                    EASTERN DIVISION

UNITED STATES OF AMERICA      )    No.   02 CR 506
                              )
                              )    Judge Rebecca Pallmeyer
                              )
         v.                   )    Violations: Title 18, United
                              )    States Code, Sections 2, 1001
LAWRENCE E. WARNER and        )    1341, 1346, 1951, 1956 and 1962
GEORGE H. RYAN, SR.           )    Title 26, United States Code
                              )    Sections 7206 and 7212; and
                              )    Title 31, United States Code, Section 5324
                              )
                              )    Second Superseding Indictment

                        COUNT ONE
```

The SPECIAL APRIL 2002 GRAND JURY charges:

1. At times material to this indictment:

   Office of the Secretary of State

   A. The Office of the Secretary of State of the State of Illinois (hereinafter "SOS Office") was entrusted with comprehensive duties relating to motor vehicles, including licensing drivers, administering and enforcing driver safety, maintaining driving records, selling and distributing license plates and vehicle registration validation stickers and issuing and maintaining records of vehicle titles. In addition, the SOS Office, through its Inspector General Department (hereinafter "IG Department"), was charged with investigating alleged misconduct by SOS Office employees.

   B. The Secretary of State, one of the elected statewide officers of the State of Illinois, was responsible for running the SOS Office, the second largest of Illinois' constitutionally-mandated offices. From 1991 through early 1999, the SOS Office employed over 3,000 employees.

1

available to the public. Prior to each filing, the income and expenditure activity was reviewed by numerous Citizens For Ryan agents, including Fawell, and then verified for truth and completeness by the treasurer of Citizens For Ryan at the time of filing.

   i. Citizens For Ryan maintained one or more bank accounts at various financial institutions in Illinois. Defendant RYAN, with the assistance of Fawell, possessed ultimate control and decision-making authority over Citizens For Ryan bank accounts. Citizens For Ryan also maintained one or more credit card accounts, and credit cards were issued to RYAN and Fawell, who utilized said credit cards, along with funds from the Citizens For Ryan bank accounts, to pay campaign and personal expenses of RYAN.

   ii. From at least 1991 through 2002, defendant RYAN routinely used Citizens For Ryan funds and credit cards to benefit himself, family members and other third parties. Generally, Illinois law permitted the expenditure of campaign funds for personal purposes, provided that the personal expenditures were reported as such on the campaign finance disclosure reports. In addition, RYAN was required by law to accurately and fully report on his federal and state income tax returns all expenditures of Citizens For Ryan funds for personal purposes.

   iii. During each of the 1994 and 1998 political campaigns involving defendant RYAN, RYAN caused substantial Citizens For Ryan funds to be set aside for personal use in the event that the respective campaigns were unsuccessful. Generally, Illinois law further permitted a former public official to use any outstanding balance in a campaign fund for personal use, provided again that the former public official accurately and fully reported on his federal and state income tax returns all such conversions of campaign funds.

   iv. At all times between December 31, 1995 and May 2002, Citizens For

January 29, 2004

A law firm (who requested confidentiality) declined to represent me in my quest to continue my legal actions. This was my last attempt to hire an attorney or law firm in this matter.

March 25, 2004

The seventh anniversary of Mom's death.

I woke in the middle of the night, thinking of her. I looked out the window and saw a beautiful moon. It was then that I decided to write this story and put closure to this chapter of my life. I was only able to write two pages.

I received another premonition, just like the others. I believed the delay in writing this story was intentional, so as to allow more data to be uncovered in regard to others who may have been responsible for of the alleged cover-up in the recall and the investigation into the hospitals' and doctors' conduct.

February 2005

I had a dream about Mom. We were walking and talking, and after our conversation, she said good-bye. The dream felt so real. It felt like a chapter was ending. I now believe, from the feelings the dream produced, that she also contacted me during my investigation.

May 11, 2005

In the news:

The indictment of Stuart Levine, the former vice chairman of the Illinois Health Facilities Planning Board, for allegedly leveraging his post on the board so that two associates could gain lucrative hospital construction and financing contracts. Levine had been on the board since December 1996. This board is part of the Illinois Department of Public Health.

Stuart Levine

Stuart Levine, a Chicago attorney, is one of the original shareholders in HMO America, Inc. He was a partner in Herman, Tannebaum & Levine, a firm specializing in health care law. He is also former president and a large shareholder of Photogen Technologies, Inc. As a member of the Illinois Gaming Board, he opposed the building of the Emerald Casino in Rosemont before he resigned from the Board in 2001. In 2003, Gov. Blagojevich appointed Levine to the Illinois Health Facilities Planning Board; he was later purged from the Board and in 2005 was indicted on charges that he acted corruptly by denying permits to hospitals that refused to hire politically connected financiers and contractors.

From January 1, 1993 to June 30, 2004, Stuart Levine gave $1.6 million to candidates for Illinois statewide constitutional and legislative office, 99% of which was contributed to Republicans.

(Illinois Campaign for Political Reform-May 2005)

Note: Illinois Department of Public Health: Stuart Levine, the former vice-chairman for the Illinois Health Facility Planning Board, was indicted in May 2005. Former Governor George Ryan appointed Mr. Levine before Gov. Blagojevich.

Author's aside: To the best of my knowledge, the Illinois Department of Public Health has yet to investigate my complaints filed in 2000. Disturbingly, former governor George Ryan reappointed Mr. Levine to this post. It appears that the existence of a "culture of corruption" may be true.

The American Genocide

U. S. Department of Justice

United States Attorney
Northern District of Illinois
Federal Building

Patrick J. Fitzgerald
United States Attorney

219 South Dearborn Street, Fifth Floor
Chicago, Illinois 60604
(312) 353-5300

FOR IMMEDIATE RELEASE
MONDAY MAY 9, 2005

PRESS CONTACT:
Randall Samborn   (312)353-5318
U.S. Attorney's Office

LEVINE, KIFERBAUM AND HURTGEN INDICTED ON FRAUD CHARGES ALLEGING KICKBACKS, INFLUENCE-PEDDLING AND INSIDER-DEALING

Hospital projects in McHenry and Will counties subjected to pay-to-play scheme

CHICAGO – Three Chicago area executives – one of them a former member of the Illinois Health Facilities Planning Board, which controls medical facility construction projects in Illinois, and one a managing director of Bear Stearns & Co., an investment firm that arranges financing for public works projects in Illinois – were indicted on federal charges for allegedly engaging in insider-dealing, influence-peddling, kickbacks and corruption involving their private interests and public duties, federal officials announced today. One defendant, **Stuart Levine**, a lawyer and businessman, allegedly engaged in a fraud scheme to obtain a total of at least $9.5 million for himself and certain associates, while the other two defendants, **Jacob Kiferbaum**, an architect and construction firm executive, and **P. Nicholas Hurtgen**, a lawyer and investment banker, allegedly participated in the same fraud scheme to obtain multi-million dollar contracts for their businesses through construction kickbacks or other fraudulent deals. Levine and Hurtgen were arrested this morning by federal agents. Kiferbaum is cooperating with the investigation and was not arrested. All three were charged with various counts of fraud and extortion in a 28-count indictment that was returned by a

Chapter 8
Conclusion

The lengthy legal battle of *Advincula v. UBS* might explain why I had little or no success fighting in court and why the chances of success in administrative proceedings were even less. That case also presents a rationale as to why so many attorneys feared a legal battle with UBS and the blood banking industry. I was surprised when, in 2004, I read a story about a yearly ceremony attended by some Illinois supreme justices and the defendant's leading law firm having a great time together. But I consider it a victory, for the victims and me, because I am able to bring this story and information to the public, expressing my rights of free speech with no intention to profit financially. If you believe in what you do and enjoy your relationship with destiny, then you will understand why I was driven to tell this story. This story was not only written for my mom, it was written for those we can't hear, those silent voices that belonged to our mothers, fathers, family members, friends, or associates who received tainted blood transfusions.

It's necessary that my readers remember the important points that led me to believe that a massacre and cover-up may have occurred.

1. There was a blood recall in the Chicagoland area (*Tribune* December 1998).

2. The Illinois Department of Public Health records indicated an increase in AIDS between 1992 and 1996.

3. Over forty thousand people were affected in the Chicagoland area (*Tribune* December 1998).

4. Individuals were indicted for allowing the blood supply to be adulterated.

5. Some of the suspected tainted blood supply was sent to several Chicagoland hospitals over a period of years and went undetected (FDA Consent Decree 1996).

6. NYBC stated, "Recall is being conducted due to our inability to assure that these products were properly tested for the viral markers and anti-HCV, anti-HBC, and HIV p24 antigen" (NYBC July 14, 1997).

7. "We recommend patients be notified if transfused with any transfusable noted on the attached anti-HCV recall list" (NYBC July 14, 1997).

8. A letter of intent to revoke their license was sent to United Blood Services (UBS) of Chicago. UBS violations included "collection of blood from unsuitable individuals and reinstatement of ineligible HIV-reactive donors" (FDA July 17–September 25, 1995).

9. A consent decree ordering the recall and correction of errors (FDA December 1996).

10. Blood Systems Inc. had duplicate donors in their computer files (FDA July 17–September 25, 1995).

11. FDA refused to turn over deleted information (FOIA Request 2001).

12. NYBC records indicate the problem was from 1991 to 1996 (FDA Consent Decree 1996).

13. Settlement offers from Blood System Inc. and Mr. Harper of South Shore Hospital (1999).

14. Illinois Department of Public Health delayed investigation of hospitals (IDPH April 2001).

15. The *Advincula* case heard at the Illinois Supreme Court during the

blood recall recommendation. The recall was announced two years later (December 1996).

16. Stuart Levine, the former vice chairman for the Illinois Health Facility Planning Board, was indicted. Former Governor George Ryan appointed him (IDPH 2005).

17. Former Governor George Ryan was quoted as saying his administration "had a culture of corruption" (December 2003).

18. Except for the first complaint against South Suburban Hospital, all the Illinois State Department agencies I had filed a complaint with "let the lawyers off the hook," didn't investigate the hospitals as they stated they would, and failed to properly investigate the doctors involved. All agencies had Governor George Ryan's name on their stationery, and he appointed the State Department heads. This was his administration.

19. The Illinois Supreme Court justice who issued the opinion in the case of *Advincula v. United Blood Services* was once under investigation by the FBI (July 2002).

20. Columbus Hospital stated Mom was diagnosed with Wegener's granulomatosis (November 1996), but their doctor didn't list it as a cause of death (March 1997) although she was under his care and on medication for Wegener's granulomatosis when she died. Columbus Hospital eventually closed down.

Chapter 9

I am hopeful that these findings will encourage you to consider the facts. If you believe a friend, or loved one, may have been affected and wish to seek answers, below are a few suggestions:

1. Ascertain if he or she received a blood transfusion between the years 1991 and 1996 or in 1997. I believe there might have been adulterated blood supply at some hospitals after 1996. If death was recent, it may have been from a similar incident.

2. Look at the blood test results before and after the transfusion. Many transfusions are also given during surgery.

3. If that person had a setback, or died after a transfusion, go a little further and look at the biopsy, autopsy, and/or death certificate for cause of death. Pay close attention to parts 1 and 2 on the death certificate.

4. If you suspect foul play, you may want to consider an expert opinion. If there was a sudden death while hospitalized, renal failure, sepsis, or suspicious infection in the blood, you might have something.

Below, find a summary of an article from a local newspaper listing hospitals in the Chicagoland area.

Hospitals affected in Chicago area

Chicago

1. Bethany Hospital
2. Children's Memorial Hospital
3. Chicago Osteopathic Hospital
4. Columbus Hospital
5. Edgewater Hospital
6. Grant Hospital
7. Louis A. Weiss Memorial Hospital
8. Mercy Hospital and Medical Center
9. Norwegian-American Hospital
10. Northwestern Memorial Hospital
11. Rush-Presbyterian-St. Luke's Medical Center
12. St. Anthony Hospital
13. St. Elizabeth's Hospital
14. St. Francis Cabrini Hospital
15. St. Joseph Hospital
16. South Shore Hospital
17. Swedish Covenant Hospital
18. University of Chicago Hospital
19. University of Illinois Medical Center

Suburbs

20. Condell Memorial Hospital, Libertyville
21. Gottlieb Memorial Hospital, Melrose Park

22. Great Lakes Naval Hospital, Great Lakes

23. Hinsdale Hospital, Hinsdale

24. Little Company of Mary Hospital, Evergreen Park

25. Midwest Regional Medical Center (formerly American International Hospital), Zion

26. Oak Park Hospital, Oak Park

27. St. Francis Hospital, Blue Island

28. Victory Hospital, Waukegan

(*Chicago Tribune*, Ken Marshall, FDA, December 2, 1998) Sources: United Blood Service, American Association of Blood Banks, LifeSource, U.S. Food and Drug Administration.

Epilogue

It is fitting to say that like most accusations, this one is legally referred to as "alleged." I am not trying to hurt anyone personally or professionally, nor am I trying to imply that anyone or any company named in this story did any wrongdoing. I merely ask you to look at the facts and draw your own conclusions.

I am recording what I experienced, heard, felt, read, and believed to have occurred. I don't believe the FDA was part of a cover-up or culture of corruption. I think the FDA did an excellent job with their investigation by means of the consent decree, indictments, inspection of blood companies, and making limited records available to the public. Agencies or bureaus that large will sometimes have difficulties communicating with each other. After reviewing the following headline, "10 On FDA Panel Tied to Drug Firms, Group Claims," I did have some concerns (AP, *Chicago Sun-Times*, February 26, 2005). This article is not related to the tainted blood, but it raises a few questions, especially if this advisory panel had a say in the delay of the recall notification or if some of its members had ties to the blood banking industry.

A quote, which seems logical, states, "It should be unethical for any judge to accept campaign donations from companies, lawyers, or law firms that have been before them in court."

I hope that one day the following questions, and many others, may be answered:

1. Was the blood recall delayed in 1996 for statute of limitation purposes or to prevent or win a lawsuit?

2. Did more adulterated blood enter the Chicagoland area than reported?

3. Were deaths or illnesses caused by adulterated blood covered-up by hospitals?

4. Did the culture of corruption prevent the Illinois Department of Public Health from investigating my complaints?

Did it influence the outcome of the doctors' and lawyers' investigations?

Throughout my attempt to find the underlying cause of this matter, not one of the defendants has yet to respond to my request in which I asked them to inform us, Mary's family, whether she had been transfused with adulterated blood from South Shore and Columbus hospitals. There were two settlement offers, one verbally, and one in writing, stating, "The settlement will require that you release all claims against Blood Systems Inc. and other parties who may be involved in this matter" (June 13, 2000).

To the best of my knowledge, no one in the state of Illinois has yet to investigate the recall delay or the cases of an estimated forty thousand patients who received blood transfusions, nor has anyone investigated my mother's circumstances.

Below are a few more items to consider before coming to a conclusion:

1. The suspected tainted blood was sent to hospitals in Chicago and other areas.
2. My mother received blood transfusions at two of these hospitals.
3. She became sick after these transfusions and subsequently died.
4. The blood recall was announced more than two years after it was detected in 1996.
5. There are motives for why the recall was delayed.
6. There are motives for why hospital boards didn't investigate.
7. On February 2, 1997, Mary was diagnosed at South Suburban Hospital with leukopenia and granulomatosis. *Wegener's granulomatosis* was later handwritten next to *granulomatosis*, which gives rise to suspicion. The consulting physician was Dr. Kumarajah, and the referring physician was Dr. Rao.
8. Leukopenia is associated with many of the viruses reported in the blood recall. Granulomatosis is associated with viral infections. Dr. Rao was treating Mom with three types of medications, according to her medical records, prior to her being admitted to South Suburban Hospital.
9. The medical journal indicated that the medicines should not be taken together. Two of the medications suppress the immune system. The medical journal stated two of the medications should not be given to a patient with kidney problems. She developed a kidney malfunction after her body was invaded by severe infections after receiving the blood transfusions.
10. She was placed on dialysis while hospitalized at Columbus Hospital.
11. Dr. Rao is from Columbus Hospital.

12. One medication treats both leukemia and Wegener's granulomatosis. Wegener's granulomatosis is a noninfectious nephritic syndrome.

13. One medication treats hepatitis. A viral infection associated with HIV, hepatitis, and leukemia was found in Mom's biopsy report.

14. The third medication treats the kidney and organ transplant rejections. The questions are the following:

Were these medications given to treat and/or cover HIV, hepatitis, or leukemia? Were the dialysis and blood transfusions at Columbus given for reasons other than those stated? Was this type of cover-up widespread? Was this genocide?

These are the questions; now we have some answers.

After a Freedom of Information Act request in August 2007, I learned that IDPH failed to investigate my mother's death, and that inactions may have caused thousands of patients in Illinois to be in the same predicament as my mom.

For example, when the IDPH statistics reported that HIV/AIDS diagnoses decreased in the mid-1990s, it is believed that HIV/AIDS types of blood transfusion infections were actually increasing; but the statistics were disguised as deaths related to nephritic syndrome and septicemia. In 1990, IDPH statistics reported there were 1,186 nephritic syndrome deaths. In 2005, IDPH statistics reported there were 2,388 nephritic syndrome deaths and 1,939 septicemia deaths. Many of these infections are believed to have been caused by adulterated blood products that were supplied by blood companies such as United Blood Service (see FDA inspection reports for UBS in Chicago, Illinois, for 1993, 1994, and 1995). An FDA blood recall was announced in Chicago on December 2, 1998. The actual recall date was December 17, 1996, as ordered by a consent decree (FDA Consent Decree 96 Civ. 9464 RPP, December 17, 1996, SDNY), which stated the blood wasn't safe as early as 1991. This recall affected over forty thousand people. These statistical numbers continue to increase every year. A calculation of deaths above the norm from 1990 to 2005 is between thirty thousand and forty thousand in Illinois. This total is similar to the number of people affected by the blood recall.

Dr. Epstein letter also supports my belief that individuals were infected with tainted blood transfusions before and after the consent decree. Excerpts from the letter of Dr. Jay S. Epstein to Judge Baer concerning *United States v. Maniago and Gonzales* that states,

> I submit this letter and attached affidavit, to bring to your Honor's attention the seriousness of the conduct of which defendants Ross Gonzales and Eliazar Maniago have been convicted.
>
> Each year more than 18 million units of blood, platelets, red blood cells, and other blood products are transfused into patients in the United States.
>
> As I am sure the evidence at the trial made clear, adulterating the viral testing of blood donations by manipulating the tests controls and blanks had the effect of making results of the viral tests in question

unreliable. As such, the conduct of which the defendants have been convicted undermined the work of the FDA and blood professionals to insure the highest possible safety of our blood supply.

The FDA has compared the viral testing data from NYBC from before the consent decree with comparable data from the NYBC generated after the entry of the consent decree. This analysis demonstrates that there is an increase in the number of initially reactive tests after the consent decree. This increase is evident for several viral tests. Briefly, we reason that the lower rate of initially reactive tests observed prior to monitoring is an effect of the adulteration.

The defendants, Maniago and Gonzales, were charged with the adulterating the blood products and found guilty. They knew their actions that were thought of beforehand would kill many Americans. The hospitals and doctors who actually covered up their patients' deaths and diagnosis that was a result of this adulterated blood committed crimes as well.

The facts will speak for themselves.

Final Note

In closing, I can't predict the future outcome for those who are guilty of a crime in this story. One important fact is that some of those that were in key positions to help tainted blood victims now and during the blood recall era failed to perform their duties according to the IDPH's recent statistics on blood poisoning. One thing I am certain of is that many of those linked directly and indirectly to this tragedy have already been punished in some way. There appears to be evidence that their punishment came from a higher level of some kind, and this powerful force will continue to pursue those responsible for their sins.

For example, a former governor was found guilty of corruption, an Illinois Department of Public Health facility planning board member plead guilty to corruption and has implicated many others in a corruption scheme, a lawyer linked to the former chief justice has several pending federal criminal charges, and Columbus Hospital closed down. A tragic auto accident also struck one of the doctor's family members, according to a newspaper article. I am convinced justice will continue to prevail. You may now understand why it is my divine appointment to tell my mom's personal story, which may be linked to current HIV/AIDS blood concerns, now affecting between 33.4 and 46 million people globally (UNAIDS, "Overview of the global AIDS epidemic," *2006 Report on the Global AIDS Epidemic*, PDF [2006]).

About the Author

E. Slaughter Sr. holds a master's degree in criminal justice and corrections from CSU, Chicago, Illinois. Slaughter has over twenty-five years of experience in criminal justice and law enforcement, including investigation training. He is a part-time consultant, community activist, and former first vice president of the Illinois Academy of Criminology and the NAACP-Chicago (WS) branch.

He is the author of *Ghosts of Hollandale* and publisher and coauthor of *Uncle Percy's Blessing* with his daughter Loni N. Slaughter.

You can contact the author for additional information by e-mail at Eslaughter3374@wowway.com or P.O. Box 314, Calumet City, Illinois, 60409.

www.ingramcontent.com/pod-product-compliance
Lightning Source LLC
Chambersburg PA
CBHW071707040426
42446CB00011B/1947